VOLUNTARY APPROACHES TO DEBT RELIEF

AF683075

POLICY ANALYSES IN INTERNATIONAL ECONOMICS 25

VOLUNTARY APPROACHES TO DEBT RELIEF

John Williamson

INSTITUTE FOR INTERNATIONAL ECONOMICS
WASHINGTON, DC
SEPTEMBER 1988

John Williamson is a Senior Fellow at the Institute for International Economics. He was formerly economics professor at Pontifícia Universade Católica do Rio de Janeiro, University of Warwick, Massachusetts Institute of Technology, University of York, and Princeton University; Advisor to the International Monetary Fund; and Economic Consultant to Her Majesty's Treasury. Williamson has published numerous studies on international monetary issues, including IMF Conditionality, The Failure of World Monetary Reform 1971–74, *and* Political Economy and International Money.

The author acknowledges with gratitude numerous invaluable comments on earlier drafts by seminar participants, referees, and colleagues; and the typing of Angela Barnes.

J.W.

INSTITUTE FOR INTERNATIONAL ECONOMICS
11 Dupont Circle, NW
Washington, DC 20036
(202) 328-9000 Telex: 261271 IIEUR Fax: (202) 328-5432

C. Fred Bergsten, *Director*
Ann L. Beasley, *Director of Publications*

The Institute for International Economics was created by, and receives substantial support from, the German Marshall Fund of the United States.

The views expressed in this publication are those of the author. This publication is part of the overall program of the Institute, as endorsed by its Board of Directors, but does not necessarily reflect the views of individual members of the Board or the Advisory Committee.

Copyright © 1988 Institute for International Economics. All rights reserved. No part of this book may be reproduced or utilitzed in any form or by any means, electronic or mechanical, including photocopying, recording, or by information storage or retrieval system, without permission from the Institute.

Printed in the United States of America 91 90 89 88 5 4 3 2 1
Library of Congress Cataloging-in-Publication Data

Williamson, John, 1937–
Voluntary approaches to debt relief/John Williamson. p. 80 cm.—(Policy analyses in international economics: 25) ''September 1988.''
Bibliography: p. 62.
1. Debts. External—Developing countries. 2. Loans. Foreign—Developing countries. 3. Debt relief—Developing countries. I. Title. II. Series.
HJ8899.W56 1988
336.3'435'091724—dc19

ISBN 0–88132–075–7 88-8397
CIP

Contents

TABLES

FIGURES

INSTITUTE FOR INTERNATIONAL ECONOMICS
11 Dupont Circle, NW, Washington, DC 20036
(202) 328-9000 Telex: 261271 IIE UR FAX: (202) 328-5432

C. Fred Bergsten, *Director*

BOARD OF DIRECTORS

Peter G. Peterson, *Chairman*
Anthony M. Solomon
Chairman, Executive Committee

Raymond Barre
W. Michael Blumenthal
Douglas A. Fraser
Alfred Herrhausen
Reginald H. Jones
Frank E. Loy
Haruo Maekawa
Donald F. McHenry
Ruben F. Mettler
Kaneo Nakamura
Suliman S. Olayan
I. G. Patel
Karl Otto Pöhl
Edmund T. Pratt, Jr.
David Rockefeller
Donna E. Shalala
Mario Henrique Simonsen
Paul A. Volcker
Louis von Planta
Dennis Weatherstone
Marina v.N. Whitman
Andrew Young

Ex officio
C. Fred Bergsten
Richard N. Cooper

Honorary Directors
Alan Greenspan
George P. Shultz

ADVISORY COMMITTEE

Richard N. Cooper, *Chairman*
Robert Baldwin
Lester R. Brown
Rimmer de Vries
Juergen B. Donges
Rudiger Dornbusch
Robert J. Flanagan
Isaiah Frank
Jacob A. Frenkel
Gottfried Haberler
Mahbub ul Haq
Arnold C. Harberger
Dale E. Hathaway
Nurul Islam
Peter B. Kenen
Lawrence R. Klein
Ryutaro Komiya
Lawrence B. Krause
Anne O. Krueger
Paul R. Krugman
Roger M. Kubarych
Robert Z. Lawrence
Assar Lindbeck
Harald B. Malmgren
Rachel McCulloch
Richard R. Nelson
Joseph S. Nye, Jr.
Rudolph A. Oswald
Jacques J. Polak
Jeffrey D. Sachs
Ernest Stern
Philip K. Verleger, Jr.
Henry C. Wallich
Alan Wm. Wolff

Preface

Debt relief has become a major policy issue as the external financial problems of a large number of developing countries continue to fester. A wide variety of proposals has been made on the topic, ranging from modest reschedulings to comprehensive writeoffs. This study is premised on the view that the modest schemes are now inadequate in many cases and that the more sweeping approaches are infeasible and perhaps undesirable. It thus primarily addresses a middle range of options, analyzing and proposing several new techniques and inducements through which the commercial lenders could voluntarily convey relief and thereby help speed a resolution of the debt problem.

This study represents a further step in the Institute's extensive work on the debt problem, which has previously included: *International Debt and the Stability of the World Economy* (1983), *International Debt: Systemic Risk and Policy Response* (1984), and *Mobilizing Bank Lending to Debt Countries* (1987) by William R. Cline; *Financial Intermediation Beyond the Debt Crisis* (1985), *Capital Flight and Third World Debt* (1987) and *Capital Flight: The Problem and Policy Responses* (1987) by Donald R. Lessard and John Williamson; and *Bank Lending to Developing Countries: The Policy Alternatives* (1985) by C. Fred Bergsten, William R. Cline, and John Williamson. In addition, Latin America's overall problems were addressed in *Toward Renewed Economic Growth in Latin America* (1986) by Bela Balassa, Gerardo M. Bueno, Pedro-Pablo Kuczynski, and Mario Henrique Simonsen.

The Institute for International Economics is a private nonprofit research institution for the study and discussion of international economic policy. Its purpose is to analyze important issues in that area and to develop and communicate practical new approaches for dealing with them. The Institute is completely nonpartisan.

The Institute was created by a generous commitment of funds from the German Marshall Fund of the United States in 1981, and now receives about twenty percent of its support from that source. In addition, major institutional grants are now being received from the Ford Foundation, the William and Flora Hewlett Foundation, and the Alfred P. Sloan Foundation. A number of other foundations and private corporations are contributing to the increasing diversification of the Institute's financial resources.

The Board of Directors bears overall responsibility for the Institute and gives general guidance and approval to its research program—including identification of topics that are likely to become important to international economic policymakers over the medium run (generally, one to three years), and which thus should be addressed by the Institute. The Director, working closely with the staff and outside Advisory Committee, is responsible for the development of particular projects and makes the final decision to publish an individual study.

The Institute hopes that its studies and other activities will contribute to building a stronger foundation for international economic policy around the world. We invite readers of these publications to let us know how they think we can best accomplish this objective.

C. FRED BERGSTEN
Director
August 1988

Voluntary Approaches to Debt Relief

1 *Introduction*

It is now six years since the debt crisis erupted with Mexico's declaration of a temporary moratorium on interest payments in August 1982. Earlier hopes that voluntary access to capital markets could be restored relatively quickly have been disappointed. No end to the crisis is in sight.

The vulnerability of the major private banks to Third World debt has been substantially reduced since 1982. Unfortunately, the situation of the debtor countries has not shown a comparable improvement. The proportion of export earnings needed to pay interest did fall when interest rates declined from the extraordinarily high levels of the early 1980s, but the ratios of debt to exports and GNP have continued to rise (although this may partly be attributable to previous underrecording of debt). The real resource transfer remains strongly negative, around $30 billion a year in 1986–87,[1] diverting savings from the investment needed to restore growth to satisfactory levels. While per capita income growth has returned to positive levels, it has not yet in general reached the rate of growth of productive potential, let alone started to make up the ground lost in the early 1980s.

In this situation, it is not surprising that proposals for reducing debt burdens continue to be advanced and even, in modest ways, implemented. Proposals for debt relief—defined as a mutually agreed reduction in the present value of future debt service obligations[2]—lie on a spectrum between those that are

1. This figure relates to all developing countries (and comes from the latest edition of the *World Debt Tables* (1988, Table 1). The comparable figures for the World Bank's 17 "highly indebted countries" that provide the primary focus of this study were $25 billion in 1986 and $20 billion in 1987 (*World Debt Tables* 1988, Table 2). The 17 highly indebted countries are Argentina, Bolivia, Brazil, Chile, Colombia, Costa Rica, Côte d'Ivoire, Ecuador, Jamaica, Mexico, Morocco, Nigeria, Peru, Philippines, Uruguay, Venezuela, and Yugoslavia.

2. The term "debt relief" is sometimes used (especially by the IMF) in a looser sense that encompasses debt rescheduling. This is unfortunate, because there is then no obvious term that makes the important distinction between debt reconstructions that reduce the present value of

mandatory and comprehensive and those that are voluntary and case-by-case. This study deals with proposals at the latter end of the spectrum, and focuses on debt held by the commercial banks.

Section 2 of this study briefly reviews the problems of more comprehensive approaches to debt relief. The analysis of "voluntary" approaches, meaning those in which each bank has the option of deciding whether or not to grant debt relief, as defined above, starts in section 3. This section is devoted to identifying the sources of potential gain from voluntary debt relief: these consist of positive incentive effects for debtor countries (summarized in the notion of a "debt relief Laffer curve") and the divergent interests of different banks. Most bankers seem to take the latter for granted, while many economists neglect or deny these divergences, so much of the argument in this section is directed at my fellow economists. Readers who accept the conclusion can skip this relatively technical section without losing the thread of the argument.

Section 4 examines alternative mechanisms for the provision of voluntary debt relief: buybacks, exit bonds, and debt/equity swaps. It compares buybacks and collateralized exit bonds and argues that the latter have little if any advantage over the former. It also discusses the forms and conditions under which uncollateralized exit bonds might be feasible, concluding that either guarantees or credible seniority would be essential. Debt/equity swaps can be useful under certain circumstances, although those circumstances would cease to exist if the remainder of the proposals developed in this study were adopted.

Section 5 deals with the design of a program of voluntary debt relief. It asks why, if section 3 is correct in arguing that there exists a strong common interest in the provision of voluntary debt relief, so little has happened until very recently. It suggests that the reasons that explain past inaction need not preclude future initiatives. Buybacks can be facilitated relatively easily, although it will be necessary for the banks to acquiesce in the provision of financial resources and grant waivers of certain traditional clauses in loan contracts. Exit bonds would require greater institutional change, since a substantial program will almost certainly require the provision of World Bank guarantees. This section also discusses the possibility of a definitive restruc-

debt-service obligations and those that do not. (A possible candidate would be "forgiveness," but this has connotations of free choice on the part of the creditors. It would seem odd to say that those banks that participated in the Bolivian buyback forgave 89 percent of their holdings of Bolivian debt.)

turing of the banks' loans, providing for automatic capitalization of interest charges above a level related to export performance, in order to supplement voluntary debt relief should the need arise.

The final section of the study tries to provide some estimate of the impact the initiatives discussed in section 5 would have on the debt problem. It concludes that buybacks alone, though helpful, could leave debtor countries under quite severe financial constraints for several years, unless, of course, improved export performance comes to the rescue. An extensive program of exit bonds has more potential, but major relief would again be delayed. Hence it may well prove desirable to supplement voluntary debt relief with a major debt reconstruction, at least for some countries, for those banks that choose not to exit.

2 *Comprehensive Schemes for Debt Relief*

It may be useful to preface a critique of schemes for comprehensive debt relief with some semantic distinctions among comprehensive, mandatory, voluntary, case-by-case, and market-oriented proposals, since all of these terms are used to describe and contrast alternative approaches.

A truly comprehensive scheme would presumably treat all loans by all creditors to all debtors in the same way. Even after one restricts "all creditors" to commercial banks and "all debtors" to the public and publicly-guaranteed (or "sovereign") debt of developing countries, it is not clear that anyone has advocated a truly comprehensive scheme. Most proposals are restricted to troubled sovereign debtors. A noncomprehensive approach on the debtor side is generally described as "case-by-case," which really means country-by-country.

A comprehensive approach on the creditor side means that all lenders to a particular debtor have their debt restructured on similar terms. Most debt restructurings to date have been comprehensive in this sense, but they have avoided granting debt relief. It is much more difficult to imagine the banks agreeing voluntarily to a comprehensive scheme that provides debt relief, which is why some schemes that aim at comprehensive relief are mandatory, meaning that they seek to compel all creditors to grant equal debt relief. However, many schemes that aim at comprehensive coverage of creditors shy away from being explicitly mandatory, and seek instead to persuade all banks to participate by weighing the scales in favor of making that choice (for example, through regulatory requirements).

The opposite of a mandatory approach is a voluntary one, in which each bank decides for itself whether to grant debt relief. The hallmark of a voluntary scheme is that different banks are expected to make different choices. In practice, voluntary schemes are virtually bound to be market-oriented, since the market establishes a price at which some potential sellers will choose to sell and others will choose not to.

Although the opposite of voluntary schemes are mandatory rather than comprehensive ones, the practical choice has been between schemes that aim to be comprehensive (even if they seek to avoid being explicitly mandatory) and those that are voluntary and aim to exploit the different interests of different banks. It is thus appropriate to contrast voluntary with "comprehensive" approaches such as those of Kenen (1983) and Rohatyn (1983), more recently Robinson (1988) and Sengupta (1988), and the congressional initiatives of LaFalce (1987) and Pease (1988).

A typical version of a comprehensive scheme proposes the creation or designation of some international agency charged with buying sovereign debt from the banks at a discount from face value in exchange for an issue of its own obligations. The agency would then lower the interest charged to the debtors (and/or extend maturities), and use the income it received from the debtors to pay the banks (while adding its guarantee that the lower level of earnings will in fact be paid). Proposals have differed enormously with respect to country coverage, the extent and variation of concessionality, mechanisms to induce participation, and so on, but the stylized proposal presented here helps to identify the critical problems inherent in a comprehensive scheme.

One problem is *inducing the banks to participate*. If the scheme provides sufficient debt relief to enable the debtor to handle its debt comfortably, then the debtor will be in a position to service in full the claims of any fringe of uncooperative banks that stand aside from the scheme. Any bank too small to believe that its individual nonparticipation will jeopardize the scheme has an incentive to act as a free rider, but the collective nonparticipation of numerous small banks could jeopardize the scheme's viability. This is the familiar free-rider problem. It is not in fact clear, however, that the principal reluctance to participate would come from the small banks: many large banks have adamantly proclaimed their unwillingness to sell at any substantial discount, in the expectation that debtor countries will ultimately recover.[3] Hence the need either to make participation mandatory or to penalize nonparticipants if reasonably comprehensive coverage of creditors is to be achieved at a price that confers a worthwhile degree of debt relief.

Legislation to compel banks to participate would seem problematical even in one country, let alone in all of the dozen or so major creditors. It is easier to imagine the penalization of nonparticipants through regulatory requirements (for example, requiring nonparticipating banks to write their loans down immediately to the value at which they would have sold them to the agency, while permitting sellers a gradual write-down).[4] The debtor might be able to help the process by treating debt bought by the agency as senior. To the extent that government authorities hesitate to employ these mechanisms with sufficient force, banks would have to be bribed to participate by use of the public purse.

A second problem is determining *how to govern country access to the debt relief facility*. This has two dimensions: how to decide which countries are covered, and how to decide the price at which the agency should buy the debt of participating countries. One surely could not limit access to the 15 countries on the Baker list, or the 17 classified as highly indebted; many other countries in equal distress have small amounts of commercial bank debt that they would certainly wish to trade in if they had the opportunity. Moreover, the availability of substantial debt relief would change the incentives facing countries (like Indonesia) that have worked hard to avoid rescheduling up to now. Popular pressure might make it difficult for the authorities of countries that do not need debt relief to resist the temptation to avail themselves of it.

3. This view is, incidentally, fully supported by the most cogent modeling available. See, in particular, Daniel Cohen (1985).

4. A conceivable alternative would be to have the IMF use its legal authority (under Article VIII, Section 2) to approve exchange controls. By making an authoritative interpretation that the disputed phrase "exchange contracts" includes international debts (an interpretation in the past rejected by US and British courts, but in which a Fund interpretation would overrule national interpretations), the Fund could give itself the right to approve the suspension or limitation of interest payments to banks located in the creditor countries. It is unclear how far this would take one, however, since legal opinions differ on whether interruptions of debt-service payments by the state (or state agencies) could be authorized in this way.

The problem of deciding the price at which such an agency should buy up the debt is also difficult. It is clear that debt could not be bought at a uniform price: the extent of relief needed in Bolivia or the Sudan would—despite the much lower level of bank exposure than in 1982—still threaten to bankrupt major banks in the United States, Great Britain, and Canada if extended to all the major debtors. Prices quoted on the secondary market might be taken as a guide, although the choice of a base date would then become a sensitive issue.

The use of secondary market prices would also raise the issue of equity: the debt of a country that has conscientiously tried to service its debts commands a higher price than that of a country that has declared interest moratoria or otherwise undermined confidence that it would strive to maintain debt service.[5] If current rather than past prices were used, an acute problem of moral hazard would arise. Requiring the banks to sell out at a price close to that quoted on the secondary market would also pose an equity issue to them. After all, insofar as the price in such a thin market measures anything, it measures the price at which they could have sold in the past, but chose not to. On the other hand, countries might resist retaining a debt substantially greater than that implied by the secondary market price, especially if they perceived their own terms to be more onerous than those of their peers. The managers of the responsible agency would, in short, have a difficult task in selecting swap prices.

Both of the preceding problems could be ameliorated by *the provision of public funds*, either in the form of cash or guarantees. Most schemes in fact call for the debt relief agency to guarantee the payment of the reduced level of debt service, which implies a guarantee for a very substantial sum, running into tens of billions of dollars each year. Many also propose a direct injection of cash.

If public funds were available for such purposes, one has to wonder whether it would be proper that they be directed to aiding the countries that overborrowed in the past, rather than to the unfortunate group of countries that were too poor ever to have been creditworthy enough to borrow. But one has to wonder even more what reason there is for supposing that public money might conceivably be made available on the requisite scale. However

5. The econometric estimates of Sachs and Huizinga (1987, 563) suggest that interest suspension depresses the secondary market price by about 17 cents on the dollar.

much one may regret it, a "Marshall Plan" for Latin America or any other region does not look like practical politics. The proposals made later in this paper, which would make bold though temporary use of the financial leeway provided by the World Bank's recent general capital increase to guarantee exit bonds, assume as much as it now seems realistic to ask the Western body politic to sanction. Drawing up plans that require even greater commitments of public funds seems unlikely to be constructive.

Admittedly, schemes for official action to force debt relief on the banks need not in principle require an input of public money. One alternative would be to establish an international tribunal empowered to organize an equivalent to "Chapter XI" proceedings for troubled sovereign debtors. I have suggested such an approach myself in the past (Williamson 1985), and Cohen (1988) has recently pursued the same line of thought. But this approach would involve a major act of institution-building, and perhaps legislation, and it is therefore out of the question unless the debt question is given a much higher political priority by Western leaders.

A final problem with negotiating a comprehensive debt relief scheme is that of *moral hazard*. This refers to the possibility that a party will be induced to modify its actions in a way that prejudices overall efficiency. In particular, if countries can qualify for significant debt relief by building up a debt burden that they cannot service or by eroding their capacity to service debt, this creates an incentive to act precisely in that way. Most schemes for debt relief seek to prevent such a response by basing the entitlement to debt relief on the circumstances existing on some date before the scheme was announced, and/or by imposing conditionality as a *quid pro quo*. But it is not clear that such solutions are totally adequate: it is doubtful that it would be possible to exclude from access to the facility a country that encountered a debt problem subsequent to the facility's establishment unless there was unambiguous evidence that the country had deliberately provoked its problem.

Moral hazard is not just a problem that affects the debtors. Creditors may also have an incentive to block solutions that recognize that the debt servicing capacity of the debtors has eroded, in the hope that they will be able to induce an input of public money. Perhaps this helps explain the banks' limited enthusiasm for innovative approaches to debt reconstruction, as well as their repeated calls for governments to play a larger role in the debt crisis. One cost of the continuing hankering after "comprehensive" solutions is that it discourages the banks from accepting the types of initiatives explored in this study.

Doubtless none of these problems would prove insuperable if there developed a strong political will either to resolve the debt crisis quickly or to protect the global financial system against an acute worsening of the debt problem precipitated by a severe world recession. The problems are nonetheless sufficiently formidable to provide ample justification for an exploration of the potential of the alternative—voluntary—approach.

3 The Logic of Voluntary Debt Relief

Unlike proposals for comprehensive debt relief, none of which have yet left the drawing board, several instances of voluntary debt relief have already occurred. The first mechanism used for this purpose was the debt/equity swap, which has been implemented in a number of countries, including Argentina, Brazil, Costa Rica, Mexico, the Philippines, and, most extensively, in Chile. In a debt/equity swap, a potential investor buys the country's debt on the secondary market and then trades it in at the central bank for local currency to use in equity investment (usually with some restrictions on remittance rights). To the extent that the central bank buys back the debt at less than 100 cents on the dollar, the country obtains a measure of debt relief.

From the standpoint of the debtor country, one unattractive feature of debt/equity swaps is that much of the benefit of the secondary-market discount goes to foreign investors rather than to itself. This is avoided with another instrument for voluntary debt relief, the buyback. Buybacks contributed significantly to the cleaning up of Latin America's debt problems in the 1930s (Eichengreen and Portes 1988; Jorgensen and Sachs 1988). At the time, one of the proponents of buybacks was a promising young economist named Henry Wallich (1943). Until recently, however, their potential relevance in helping resolve the present debt crisis has been almost entirely overlooked. The first extensive discussion can be found in Portes (1987). A substantial volume of private Mexican debt is believed to have been bought back over several years, but the first actual buyback of sovereign debt (so far as is known) was made by Bolivia in March 1988.

With the approval of the International Monetary Fund (IMF), Bolivia bought back some 47 percent of its commercial bank debt at a price of 11 cents on the dollar, using funds specially donated for this purpose by friendly governments. It was emphasized that this did not constitute a precedent. And

Bolivia is indeed a very special case. It is the second-poorest country in the Western Hemisphere and has the highest debt/export ratio. It has undertaken the most sweeping liberalization of a previously over-regulated economy, halted a hyperinflation, and suffered a collapse in the price of its principal legitimate export (tin), all while still combating the drug trade and restoring democracy. All actions create precedents, whatever declarations to the contrary are made, but Bolivia's situation was so special that the precedent was surely minimal.

The same can hardly be said of Mexico. Yet the US Treasury endorsed Mexico's plan for swapping debt into bonds whose principal is collateralized by zero-coupon US Treasury securities. Even though bankers did not bid for those bonds on a large scale on terms that the Mexicans found acceptable (and the analysis in the appendix suggests that this was to be expected), the blessing of the proposal by the US Treasury has altered the parameters of the debt crisis. Debt relief is no longer a taboo subject: the questions are whether, under what circumstances, and how it should be legitimized.

The case for legitimizing debt relief rests on two propositions. The first is that debtors are unable to fulfill their contractual obligations and therefore need cash-flow assistance either in the form of debt relief—a scaling down of those obligations—or "liquidity relief"—a postponement of a part of those obligations (which can be accomplished by the provision of "new money," among other things). The second is that banks have very different preferences with respect to the form of relief they provide, and that even those that prefer to provide liquidity relief can expect to benefit if the desires of those that would prefer to provide debt relief are accommodated. These two assertions are elaborated below.

THE NEED FOR CASH-FLOW RELIEF

So long as a country has voluntary access to the international capital market or holds more than minimal working balances in the form of international reserves, it is in a position to meet its contractual debt-service obligations irrespective of its trade balance, either by increasing its foreign liabilities or by drawing on its foreign assets. Conversely, once a country has lost voluntary access to the international capital market and drawn down its excess reserves—which has by and large been the situation of the highly indebted countries since 1982—its ability to service debt is constrained by the trade surplus it can generate. Strictly speaking, the constraint is provided by the balance on goods, services, and transfers, plus any net inflow of direct and official investment, minus the service of any senior debt (for example, to multilateral development banks [MDBs]). This may be referred to as "the surplus available for debt service," or, more briefly, the "surplus."

The following analysis requires some assumptions about the future path of this surplus, and also of the debt-service obligations. The procedure adopted here will be to start with simple but unrealistic assumptions whose implications are easy to see, and then relax these assumptions to recognize progressively more complex, but realistic, situations.

The simplest possible assumptions are that both the surplus and the debt-service obligations are fixed at some known exogenous level and are constant over all future time. In this case the country is solvent and can pay all its creditors in full if and only if the surplus exceeds the contractual debt-service obligations.[6] In the converse case, it is insolvent and some or all creditors must necessarily receive less than their contractual entitlement. Debt relief is inevitable and liquidity relief is pointless; postponement of obligations is simply a denial of the reality that the country cannot afford to pay what it owes.

Suppose one retains the assumption that debt-service obligations are fixed at some known, exogenous, and constant level (an assumption that is approximately true when debt is repeatedly rescheduled but no new money is available), but modifies the assumption concerning the surplus available for debt service. Specifically, suppose that the surplus is known and exogenous but may vary over time. Whether the country is solvent or insolvent is again well-determined (provided, at least, that the interest rate faced by the country is also known and exogenous). If the surplus grows faster than the rate of interest, then we have the case of the solvent but illiquid debtor that can service its debt provided that it gets liquidity relief.[7] Debt relief would provide

6. Let S_t be the surplus available for debt service in year t and B_t be the debt service obligation due in year t. The condition for solvency is $\int_0^\infty S_t e^{-it} dt > \int_0^\infty B_t e^{-it} dt$, where i is the interest rate. For $S_t = S$ for all t, $B_t = B$ for all t, this degenerates to $S > B$.

7. In terms of the inequality in footnote 6, a constant level of B_t guarantees that the right-hand side is finite, while S_t growing faster than i implies that the left-hand side is infinite. (This is an overly strong condition for solvency, but one that is familiar from the debt literature.)

a perfectly acceptable form of cash-flow relief from the debtor's standpoint, although it would obviously be less advantageous to the creditors.

Paul Krugman (1988a) has raised the question of why such a country should ever be illiquid: if it will ultimately be able to service its debt, it should have no difficulty in borrowing to tide it over the interim period. The answer is that two of the assumptions adopted up to this point are unrealistic—the assumptions that the path of the surplus is known with certainty and that it is exogenous.

Consider first the case of uncertainty, but simplify again by assuming that the probability distribution of the surplus is constant over time. If the mean μ of this probability distribution is less than the debt-service obligation (B_1 in figure 1a, for example), then the country is insolvent and debt relief will be needed sooner or later. If the mean exceeds the debt-service obligation (B_2 in figure 1b), but the actual outcome is less in a period when the country has no reserves, the debtor is solvent but illiquid. Liquidity relief would enable it ultimately to service its debt in full. If the bankers knew for certain that the country was solvent, they would again have no reason to deny the debtor new loans to tide it over. But this is not known with certainty. So long as there is a positive probability that the debtor is solvent, it is in the *collective* interest of the banks to provide liquidity relief rather than debt relief. However, it is in the *individual* interest of each creditor that the liquidity relief be provided by *other* creditors, so as to avoid inadvertently providing debt relief if it turns out that the creditor is really not solvent after all. Hence the free-rider problem.

In reality, the probability distribution of the surplus is not only uncertain but changes over time. In particular, views may differ on the likelihood that the probability distribution will tend to move to the right over time and, if so, whether it will move to the right faster or slower than debt service is growing as a result of interest compounding. Clearly this conjunction of circumstances provides ample scope for the situation in which it is in the collective interest of the banks to provide liquidity relief, and thus maintain the option of ultimate full recovery of their claims if circumstances turn out to be favorable, but in which this outcome is sufficiently uncertain to give each bank (and especially those with more pessimistic expectations) a strong incentive to liquidate its exposure if this is possible without undue loss.

The final assumption that needs to be relaxed is that the surplus available for debt service is exogenous with respect to the country's own actions. Clearly this assumption is useful only as an intermediate analytical tool: if it

FIGURE 1 **Frequency distribution of expected surplus**

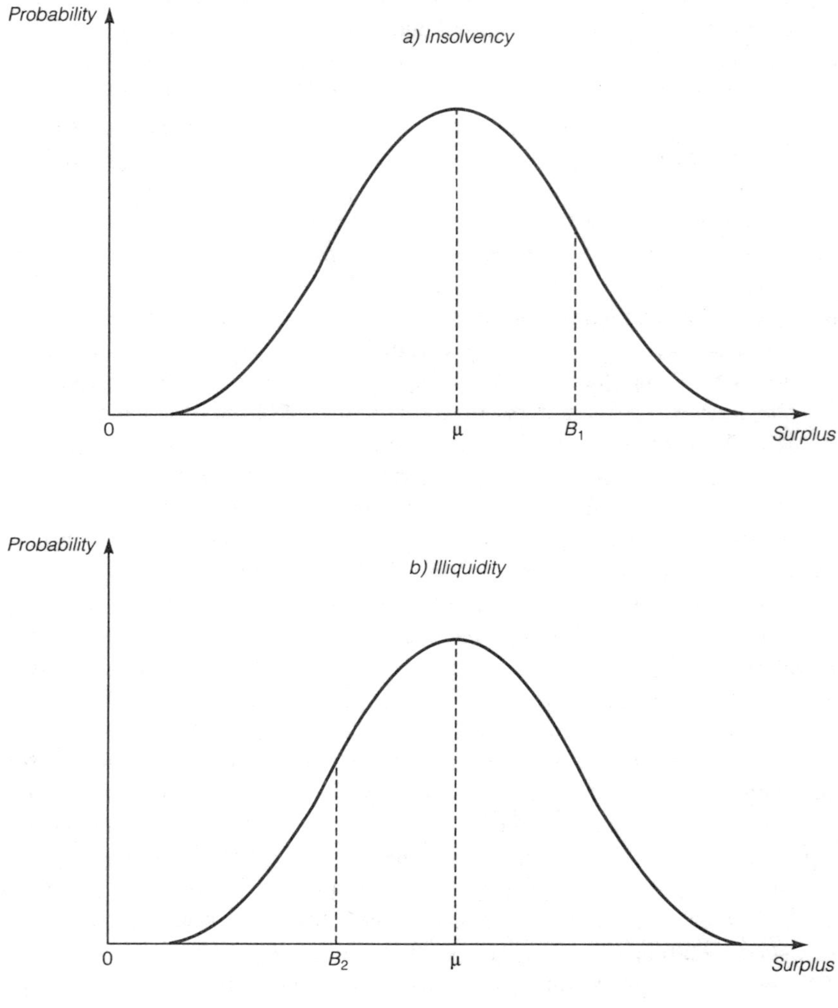

were literally true, it would imply that a debtor country was unable to benefit from debt relief by increasing its imports!

In fact, there is rarely, if ever, any relevant absolute limit on a sovereign debtor's ability to service debt. The relevant limit is set by the sacrifices that it is ethically tolerable or politically wise to impose on the populace.[8] Just how great a sacrifice should be imposed at any time is a subject on which the views of creditors and debtors can be expected to differ. The desire of creditors to ensure that their interests are not neglected tends to lead to the "short-leash approach," a preference for repeated reschedulings rather than definitive debt reconstruction, and tight conditionality. Recognition of the endogenous nature of the size of the surplus does not, however, mean that situations do not arise in which creditors have to provide either debt relief or liquidity relief. It simply means that the total amount of cash-flow relief that is needed will to some extent be a subjective variable about which creditors and debtors will typically have differing views.

It is not necessarily true that creditors have an interest in minimizing the debtors' cash-flow relief. The Baker Plan is based on the recognition that inadequate cash flow can thwart a debtor country's ability to adjust by growing out of its difficulties. Creditors have a collective interest in making this possible by the provision of liquidity relief, even though each individual creditor might prefer to reduce its exposure.

It can be argued, however, that simply affording a country the *opportunity* of adjustment-with-growth by providing it with an adequate cash flow to invest in export-generating projects may not suffice to ensure that it will actually exploit those opportunities. A major purpose of conditionality is to help ensure that debtors provided with additional foreign exchange do indeed use it for appropriate investments rather than for increased consumption. But conditionality should not be expected to persuade a country to act in a manner contrary to what it perceives as its national interest. The constructive role of conditionality is to provide financial muscle to that group of a country's decisionmakers that is urging that policy be based on what is good for the country in the long haul rather than what is politically easy in the short run. The precondition for conditionality to be able to secure an appropriate growth-oriented strategy is therefore that such a strategy actually be in the long-term interest of the country. It has been argued that this need not always be true, because of disincentive effects. Where these are sufficiently powerful, creditors and debtors may share a common interest in debt relief.

8. A more extreme view than that suggested here is adopted by Eaton, Gersovitz, and Stiglitz (1986, 485), who deny the importance of capacity to pay in constraining debt service ("[in] international loans . . . the resources of the debtor are likely to be adequate to repay the loans regardless") and conclude that willingness to pay—the "enforcement problem"—is central.

THE DEBT RELIEF LAFFER CURVE

Such an argument was raised by Bergsten, Cline, and Williamson (1985, 169), in criticism of the proposal that debt-service payments should be limited to a specified proportion of exports. The authors pointed out that this would constitute "a disincentive to export expansion, operating like an export tax." The disincentive effect of this formula would be larger if the excess of contractual obligations over the payments implied by the formula were to be forgiven rather than capitalized.

It has been claimed subsequently by Sachs (1986, 1988) and Krugman (1988a, 1988b) that a similar, but more powerful, disincentive effect can arise from the existence of an unmanageably large external debt.[9] An admirable summary of the argument is provided by Krugman:

> When a country's obligations exceed the amount it is likely to be able to pay, these obligations act like a high marginal tax rate on the country: if it succeeds in doing better than expected, the main benefits will accrue, not to the country, but to its creditors. This fact discourages the country from doing well at two levels. First, the government of a country will be less likely to be willing to take painful or politically unpalatable measures to improve economic performance if the benefits are likely to go to foreign creditors in any case. Second, the burden of the national debt will fall on domestic residents through taxation, and importantly through taxation of capital; so the overhang of debt acts as a deterrent to investment.
>
> Over and above these costs to potential repayment is the fact that no clean Chapter XI proceeding exists for sovereign debtors, and a confrontational and disorderly default may reduce the actual receipts to a creditor below what could have been obtained if debt had earlier been reduced to a level that could have been paid.
>
> The upshot of these negative effects is that the higher is the external debt of a country, the larger the probability of nonpayment; and thus the greater the subjective discount on that debt. If debt is high enough, further increases in the level of debt may actually lead to a *smaller* expected value of payments (1988b, 9–10).

Krugman illustrates the relationship between the level of debt and a creditor's expectations in terms of a diagram, reproduced in figure 2. The

9. See also the formalization of Corden (1988). In addition, Cohen (1988) has explored a different rationale that leads to the same conclusion. He argues that the present creditor strategy, which he characterizes as a hard-nosed attempt to extract full contractual debt service, risks provoking the debtors into a confrontation from which both will lose. He concludes that enlightened creditor self-interest demands partial debt forgiveness to preempt this danger.

FIGURE 2 **The debt relief Laffer curve**

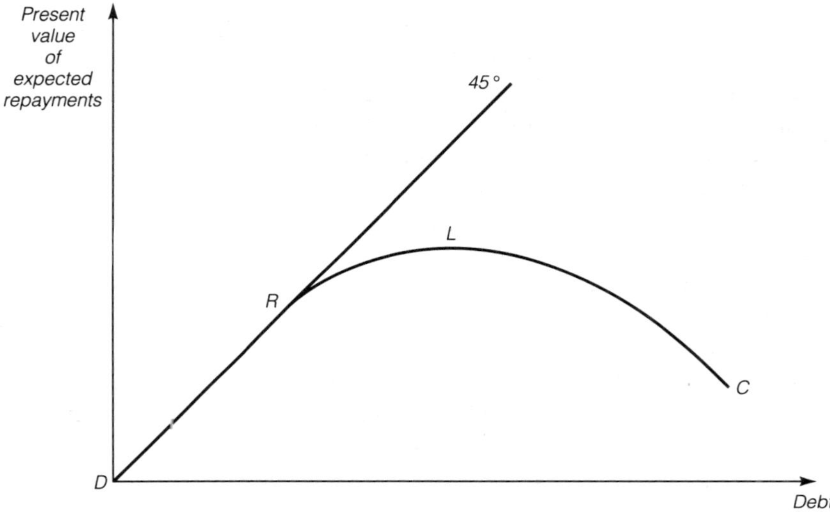

horizontal axis shows the level of debt and the vertical axis shows the expected present value of repayments. For low levels of debt from *D* to *R*, full repayment is expected, and so the outcome lies along the 45° line. At higher levels of debt, however, the possibility of nonpayment arises and grows, so that the expected payment line traces out a curve that falls increasingly below the 45° line. Beyond some point (*L*), the disincentive effects outlined above begin to outweigh the option value to the creditors of being able to share in the debtor's good fortune, should outcomes prove unexpectedly favorable. Krugman explains:

> The curve DRLC should by now be a familiar sort of object. It is the *Debt Relief Laffer Curve*. That is, just as governments may sometimes actually increase tax revenue by reducing tax rates, creditors may sometimes increase expected payment by forgiving part of a country's debt. In both cases the proposition that less is more depends on an initial extreme situation, whether of taxes that provide extreme disincentives or of a debt burden that is crippling in its effect on economic growth. Arguments that debt relief is in everyone's interest are, in effect, arguments that countries are on the wrong side of the debt relief Laffer curve (1988b, 11–12).

Two qualifications to this argument must be acknowledged. First, except under the most extreme circumstances (perhaps those of the Sudan rather than of any major Latin American debtors), countries will place some value on the reduction in their external debt that will result from enhanced export revenue. It is not *just* increased import capacity that policymakers value. Second, even if they do value additional import capacity more highly than an equivalent reduction in debt, increased export revenue will not normally be taxed away at 100 percent. Indeed, until the next new money package is negotiated, the implicit tax rate is zero. With multiyear new money arrangements there can thus be a substantial period during which all additional export revenue is available to the country.

Nonetheless, the fact remains that new money packages have to be based on an estimate of the financing gap, and it is virtually unavoidable that past success in increasing exports will be translated into a lower estimate of the future financing gap. (The position is even more clear where new money is given to clear past arrears.) This implies a high marginal "tax rate" on increased exports in the long run, almost inevitably a much higher rate than that implicit in a link between debt-service payments and export revenues. This is bad supply-side economics.

Ize and Ortiz (1987) have pointed out that a similar result may occur through a different channel. One factor that impedes the repatriation of flight capital is the fear of domestic wealth owners that an excessive level of external debt may force their government to take measures that jeopardize the value of local assets (for example, high taxation, inflation, or even expropriation). A measure of formal debt relief might ease these fears and thus improve the prospects that capital would return, which would in turn facilitate continued payment of the lower contractual level of debt-service payments.

Hence one reason that debt relief may benefit creditors is that it may improve the incentive structure facing the debtors. But this is not the only reason.

DIFFERING BANK PREFERENCES

The other reason is that the preferences of banks may differ. Some may prefer to liquidate their exposure or make it less risky, even at the cost of a substantial reduction in the present value of their contractual entitlements. Others may prefer to maintain the present value of their claims and provide liquidity relief instead of debt relief. Both groups may gain *ex ante*, according to their own preferences, if the former group is accommodated.

This proposition may be demonstrated with an arithmetical example, which is a modified version of that presented in Krugman (1988b, 14–17).[10] Consider a country that has foreign exchange reserves of 10 and debt service of 100 due in the next period. Suppose that it faces two possible outcomes, a "bad" state in which it will generate a foreign-exchange surplus available for debt service of 20, and a "good" state in which the surplus will be 80. Suppose also that 20 percent of the debt is held by "pessimists," who attach a probability of 2/3 to the bad outcome and 1/3 to the good outcome, while the remaining 80 percent is held by "optimists," who believe that the probability of the bad outcome is only 1/3 and that of the good outcome is 2/3.

If there is no buyback, the country will have available for debt service 30 in the bad state (the surplus of 20 plus the initial reserves of 10) and 90 in the good state (80 plus 10). Assuming risk neutrality, the pessimists will value this debt service at 2/3 (30) + 1/3 (90) = 50, while the optimists will value it at 1/3 (30) + 2/3 (90) = 70.

Suppose instead that the country uses its reserves of 10 to buy back the 20 of debt held by the pessimists at the price of 50 at which they value it (plus epsilon, to persuade them to sell and ensure that they too are better off after the buyback). Then in the bad case the remaining creditors will get 20, while in the good case they will get 80 (full debt service), so that they will value their remaining 80 percent of the debt at:

$$[(1/3)\ 20 + (2/3)\ 80]/0.8 = 75,$$

an improvement of 5 (minus epsilon) over the valuation without buyback.[11] Intuitively, what has happened is that the country has bought out the pessimists

10. Krugman's example was used to claim the converse, namely that buybacks could be in the interest of the creditors who did not sell out only if the country was on the wrong side of the debt relief Laffer curve. He assumed, however, that all banks hold identical views. Unfortunately, relaxing that assumption alone does not allow one to show the potential gain to the remaining creditors in his particular example because that was constructed so that they in any event get full repayment in the "good case." Since it was necessary to modify his example, other numbers have also been changed to make for less messy arithmetic.

11. If the reader wonders why this looks different from the formulae in the preceding paragraph, the answer is that they contained comparable implicit terms that cancelled. Thus the optimists' valuation of their receipts without buybacks is:

$$[(1/3)\ 30\ (0.8) + (2/3)\ 90\ (0.8)]/0.8 = 70.$$

at a price which the optimists (and presumably the country) believe to be unrealistically low, thereby leaving those who remain better off. When the good outcome is in any event not good enough to ensure full repayment, it is the optimists who reap the benefit. When (as in Krugman's original example) the good outcome is in any event good enough to finance full debt service, it is the country that gains. (Its welfare is unchanged in the example given. In both cases it uses its reserves and its surplus for debt service.) When, as generally occurs in reality, the potential outcomes straddle both possibilities, both parties may gain.

We thus have a second potential source of gain for those banks that remain. (Note that the good and bad outcomes were exogenous in the example—i.e., we abstracted from the incentive effects whose results are portrayed by the debt relief Laffer curve.) Its existence depends on banks in fact being willing to sell out at very different prices.

It is well known that the secondary market for bank loans is extremely thin. The market scarcely existed prior to the debt crisis. It has been expanding rapidly since, but the estimated 1987 turnover of something over $10 billion is still small relative to the stock of outstanding debt. The thinness of the market reflects a lack of demand. Most transactions take the form of swaps rather than sales. The demand for loan purchases is limited to foreign investors wishing to take advantage of debt/equity swaps, to the occasional bank wanting to on-lend to local clients, and to the odd company seeking to prepay local-currency liabilities cheaply. A bank that is determined to sell its loans has to be prepared to push the price down. One advantage of debtor buybacks is, of course, that they would add to demand and could thus speed the exit of banks that are not prepared to stay in for what may prove a very long haul.

The willingness of some banks to sell at a distress price implies little about the value placed on loans by other banks. It is indeed difficult to imagine that most banks anticipate receiving on average (after netting out new money) only 50 percent of the interest owed by Mexico, but that is what is implied by the recent price of Mexican debt (see the appendix).

Several reasons may account for the apparent large discrepancies in the value attached to LDC loans by different banks. Probably the most important is their differing views regarding the future prospects of the debtor countries, the factor emphasized in the preceding discussion.

This is not, however, the only possible reason. For example, the earlier analysis of the future path of a debtor's surplus available for debt service started off by considering two cases in which there was no room for differing opinions on the part of banks because the future path of the surplus was assumed to be known with certainty. Banks might nonetheless have different attitudes regarding their willingness to lend if they used different discount rates in weighing the future.

Several institutional factors are probably more important than different discount rates, though less important than differing views of the future path of the surplus, in motivating some banks to be more willing than others to sell their loans with large discounts (or otherwise exit with a sacrifice of present value). One arises from the existence of loan management costs. The legal documentation involved in rescheduling and lending new money to sovereign debtors is complex, and the cost of reviewing and processing it is much the same whether a bank has one hundred thousand or one hundred million dollars of exposure. Banks with very small exposures thus have a strong incentive to sell off their loans on the secondary market (or seek other forms of exit) even if the price is so low as to imply substantial debt relief. This is reinforced by a widespread belief that the stock market "rewards" banks that are able to declare that they no longer hold any Latin American debt.

A second reason arises from differing corporate strategies. Some banks are heavily committed to maintaining relationships with certain debtor countries, even to the point of owning a local bank with a network of branches. Such banks will be far more reluctant to sell their sovereign loans than those that have no other relationship to the country in question (although banks with a close involvement may also have opportunities denied to other banks for changing the form of their relationship through debt/equity swaps).

A third reason arises from the fact that banks are domiciled in different countries, each of which has a distinct taxation and supervisory regime. Required reserves are much higher in some countries (e.g., Sweden) than in others (e.g., Japan). The debtors against whom banks are required to hold reserves also differ from one creditor country to another. And the tax deductibility of specific and general provisions against sovereign loans varies greatly among creditor countries, with Germany and Switzerland perhaps the most generous and Japan and Singapore at the other extreme. Such differences give some banks stronger incentives to sell certain loans than other banks have, and so the prices at which different banks are willing to sell will vary.

A fourth reason is that the financial strength of banks varies, partly as a consequence of the international differences noted in the previous paragraph.

Some have adequate reserves, either general or country-specific, to enable them to sell loans on the secondary market without financial embarrassment, should that seem to them wise. Others may be constrained from action that would weaken their balance-sheet position, even if that appears to them to be the rational course.

Economists will tend to ask: if some banks really believe that loans are worth substantially more than their secondary market value, why do they not enter the market and buy these bargains? Why do we not observe buy-outs? The principal reason would seem to be that most of the optimistic banks are already overexposed. A bank may refuse to sell its existing loans at a price that it regards as far below their true value, but still feel that it would be imprudent to add further to its exposure. An additional reason might be a fear that claims bought on the secondary market would appear less legitimate than the original loans, possibly undermining the willingness of the debtor to make the sacrifices needed to maintain debt service (Rotberg 1988, 8).

Before one concludes that voluntary debt relief is in everyone's interest, one must recognize that it will not always be in the *debtor's* interest. Debt buybacks (and some other methods of voluntary debt relief—see section 4) involve the use of reserves. When a country's output and investment levels are constrained by a shortage of foreign exchange, it is entirely possible that reserves would be better used for expanding domestic investment than for extinguishing foreign debt (a point made forcefully and elegantly by Froot 1988). In judging whether or not buybacks are the best use of available reserves, a country will need to take into account both the secondary market price at which it can buy back its debt and whether it is foregoing marginal domestic investment projects that would be net generators of foreign exchange. With a discount of 50 percent, the return (entirely in foreign exchange) may be calculated as 18 percent (given a nominal interest rate of about 9 percent), suggesting that buybacks would be quite an attractive use of foreign exchange.

This calculation would not be accepted by Dooley (1988a, 1988b) or Bulow and Rogoff (1988), whose central argument can be presented in terms of figure 2.[12] The *average* cost of debt, which is what they argue a country must pay to buy back its debt on the secondary market, is given by a ray

12. Figure 2 is being used simply to portray the relationship between the level of the debt and the return investors expect from holding it. These authors do not acknowledge the incentive effects that may lead to the downward-sloping segment *LC*, but rather emphasize the positive but diminishing option value of holding higher levels of debt. This leads to a positive but flattening slope, as in the segment *RL*.

from *D* to (say) *L*. The saving of debt service that results is given by the slope of the curve *DRLC*, the "*marginal* cost of debt," which at point *L* is zero. In this case the whole benefit of the buyback thus accrues to the creditor, while the debtor has benefits less than the cost at any point to the right of *R*. The distinction between the average and marginal cost of debt arises when the new money needed in "bad" states of the world amounts to a permanent partial forgiveness of interest, rather than its postponement. This is clearly a possible outcome, but those who do not regard it as a central expectation will conclude that the distinction between the average and marginal cost of debt is not of great import.[13] On the other hand, this analysis abstracts from both of the factors cited above to justify the belief that buybacks can bring mutual gain—the incentive effects summarized in the debt relief Laffer curve (which imply that a gain to the banks is not necessarily a loss to the country) and the differing views of different banks (which imply that the cost of a buyback is likely to be less than the average cost of debt).

The marginal–average distinction does suggest that the return to buybacks may be less than implied by the formula (interest saving) ÷ (one minus discount), especially for countries whose debt trades at a high discount. However, it will not be drastically less except in the case of a country the nominal value of whose debt is of no consequence in determining its debt-service obligation. Most countries should find the returns on buybacks and other exit vehicles attractive.

4 Alternative Mechanisms for Voluntary Debt Relief

The most straightforward mechanism for securing voluntary debt relief is the *buyback*. Its disadvantage is that it requires a debtor to have in hand the foreign exchange to buy its debt on the secondary market.

13. Bulow and Rogoff (1988) also point to the Bolivian buyback as evidence. Bolivian debt rose from a price of 6 cents on the dollar, before a buyback was rumored, to 11 cents after it had taken place, resulting in a minimal fall in the total market value of Bolivian debt. They interpret this as implying that the market had an unchanged view of the level of debt service that Bolivia could and would pay, which the buyback simply spread over a smaller number of claims. My interpretation is different: that the buyback resulted in the elimination of the most pessimistic holders. Buying these out could be advantageous to Bolivia even if the result was to *increase* the total market value of its debt, which does not reflect (and still less determines) Bolivia's short-run payments, which are zero, but rather the date at which payments are expected to resume. By advancing that date and reducing the cost of resuming payment the buyback has benefited both the nonexiting banks and Bolivia.

An alternative approach is to swap, or defease,[14] loans into *exit bonds*. An exit bond was defined in Bergsten, Cline, and Williamson (1985, 181) as "a long-term bond carrying a low interest rate, which would bestow on the purchaser the right of exemption from participation in further rescheduling and coordinated lending exercises. These bonds would not themselves be rescheduled, nor would they be counted as a part of the base that determines the obligation to put up new money."

This definition is too narrow because it takes for granted that debt relief has to be given via a concessional interest rate, whereas the Mexican precedent showed that it could also be provided by new bonds being swapped with outstanding loans at a discount from face value. In the Mexican case, for example, existing bonds were traded in at an average discount of 30 percent, so that $1 of new bonds replaced $1.43 of old loans, but the interest rate on the new bonds is actually slightly higher. The only previous attempt to issue exit bonds, by Argentina in mid-1987, involved swapping at par, a concessional interest rate of 4 percent, 25 years' maturity, and 12 years' grace. Only five banks elected to take bonds on those terms.

One broad distinction among exit bonds is thus whether they provide the concession to the debtor in terms of the interest rate or in terms of the value of the bond issue. But the more important question is whether they carry guarantees or other forms of "credit enhancement." If so, these guarantees may apply to either the principal or the interest payments or both; they may be partial or total; and they may be provided either by some outside benefactor or by the country buying financial assets to serve as collateral. The Mexican bond issue carried a total guarantee of the principal provided by Mexican purchases of US Treasury zero-coupon securities with a maturity identical to that of the Mexican bond issue (20 years).

To the extent that exit bonds are neither guaranteed by an outside agency nor collateralized, the question arises as to whether their interest and/or principal payments are senior to those on existing loans. The seniority of interest was left obscure in the case of the Mexican defeasance scheme. Morgan Guaranty and the US Treasury apparently assured the banks that the new loans would not be senior, while Mexican officials reportedly stated the contrary. Any such seniority could only represent a policy intention by the authorities, since no request was made for legal subordination of existing

14. Defeasance is defined as the replacement of one bond issue by another.

debt—a request that would have required approval by every creditor bank. Such intentions cannot provide a completely credible guarantee to the creditor, whatever the commitments of the debtor, owing to the sharing clause, which entitles all creditors to share equally any disproportionate payments they may receive. This clause could provide the basis for a legal challenge by disgruntled banks to the banks that had bought exit bonds if other loans were not being serviced.

Apart from buybacks and exit bonds, the third channel for voluntary debt relief is the conversion of loans into *local currency for equity investment.* This usually involves restrictions on the right to remit profits for several years, and even longer restrictions on the right to sell out and remit the capital. The central bank typically buys back the loans below par, thus capturing a part of the secondary market discount. The price at which it buys the debt back has sometimes been determined by an auction.

It would doubtless be possible to conceive of intermediate proposals. For example, loans might be converted at a discount into bonds whose future debt-service payments would be paid in local currency to be used for equity investment. However, the alternatives identified above would seem to provide an adequate basis for analysis.

In addition, there may be possibilities for mutually beneficial debt reconstruction that do not involve debt relief, but that seek instead to rearrange payments obligations with reference to exogenous contingencies. The leading example is commodity-linked bonds. These might, for example, cut the interest rate due unless the price of some major export commodity rose beyond some threshold, above which the interest rate could rise progressively until it was higher than the present contractual rate. If the terms of such a bond were chosen so that the expected present value of contractual payments did not diminish, no debt relief would be involved. The author has already argued in favor of such proposals (Lessard and Williamson 1985), but they will not be considered further in the present study.

OPTIMAL USE OF RESERVES

Several issues arise in choosing among these alternatives. A first is whether the country has foreign exchange available. If it does, then it has the option of buying back debt on the secondary market or issuing bonds whose debt service is at least in part collateralized, in addition to the options available to countries that do not have spare reserves (analyzed subsequently). Before committing itself to the use of foreign exchange to buy back loans or collateralize bonds, the debtor will need (as noted in section 3) to assure itself that this is a better use of foreign exchange than the import of investment goods to increase domestic capital formation. This will depend both on the size of the discount on the secondary market and the rate of return on additional domestic investment.

The appendix contains a detailed comparison between buybacks and defeasance on the Mexican model, involving collateralization of the principal. It is also possible to conceive of a country placing funds in an escrow account in order to collateralize a part of the interest.

The appendix shows that under certain assumptions a banker's choice between holding on to loans, swapping into principal-collateralized bonds, and selling on the secondary market depends on two critical variables, *b* and *p* in figure 3. The variable *b* on the vertical axis is the "bid price" for a loan/bond swap—the number of cents on the dollar at which a bank offers to swap its existing loans for defeased bonds. (The average value of *b* for the bids that Mexico accepted was 0.7—i.e., 70 cents of new bonds were issued for each dollar of old loans.) The variable *p* on the horizontal axis is the probability that the banker attaches to interest on outstanding loans actually being paid in any period. (It is assumed that this probability is constant in each future period, but a variant on this assumption considered in the appendix provides some reassurance that the results presented below are not sensitive to this specification.)

Clearly the choice between holding on to loans and selling on the secondary market does not depend on *b,* so the boundary between those two alternatives is a vertical line. In fact, it is a vertical line at that probability *p* equal to the price on the secondary market. That is, any bank that estimates that the probability of receiving interest in any future year is less than the price on the secondary market will prefer to sell off its loans, while any bank that thinks the probability is higher will prefer to retain its loans. It seems rather extraordinary that banks should regard the probability of receiving interest from Mexico in any future year as no better than 50 percent, but this is what the secondary market price of 50 cents on the dollar implies. However, that is also the price at which most banks have chosen *not* to sell, which makes it clear why they would have a legitimate grievance if some mandatory scheme were to oblige them to sell out at or near that price.

FIGURE 3 **Bankers' preferences among retaining loans, swapping into collateralized bonds, and selling on the secondary market.**

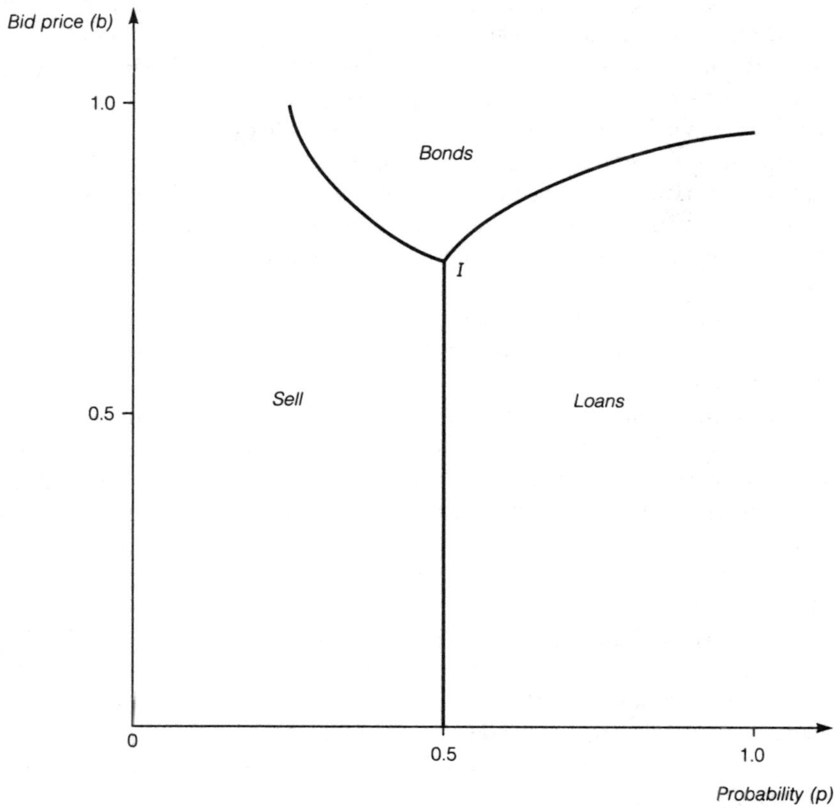

If the country is willing to offer a swap into collateralized bonds at a sufficiently good rate (i.e., high value of b), then such a swap will be preferable either to sale on the secondary market or to retention of existing loans (figure 3). If interest on bonds is senior to that on existing loans, this will tend to expand the area where bonds dominate in figure 3 by reducing the vertical height of the intersection point I, flattening the boundary between the "bonds" and "sell" segments, and steepening the boundary between the "bonds" and "loans" segments. In the limit, if interest on the bonds were judged to be free of default risk, the boundary between the "bonds" and "sell" segments would be horizontal. If the interest rate were identical on the defeased bonds and on the old loans, the vertical coordinate (b) would be identical to the horizontal coordinate (p). When, as in the Mexican scheme, the interest rate on bonds is higher than that on loans, it would actually pay a bank to bid a price (b) *lower* than that at which it could sell on the secondary market in order to switch into bonds.

The attractiveness to the debtor of securing a switch from loans into bonds depends on how low a price (b) the banks will bid to get rid of their loans, and also (inversely) on the size of any premium on the interest spread on bonds as opposed to loans. In addition, the defeasance alternative tends to appear more attractive to the debtor when the social discount rate it uses to discount foreign exchange is relatively low.[15] Clearly the option of buybacks tends to appear more attractive the lower is the price on the secondary market.

When one combines the analysis of the interests of the creditors and the debtors, it emerges that there are two circumstances which can cause defeasance to appear preferable to buybacks. One is when the banks believe that interest payments on the defeased bonds carry seniority over those on loans; this can motivate a bank to make an attractive (low) bid b to swap into bonds. The other is when the debtor discounts foreign exchange at a relatively low rate.

The analysis in the appendix shows that, given that the bankers appear to have attached little credence to Mexican assurances that interest on the collateralized bonds would be treated as senior, the Mexican approach was more cost-effective than buybacks would have been only for discount rates below 14 percent. This is on the low side for plausible estimates of social discount rates for foreign exchange in payments-constrained countries, suggesting that buybacks are probably (though not unambiguously) a more cost-effective use of foreign exchange. The one factor that could clearly tilt the advantage toward bonds is seniority.

15. This is because the bulk of the pecuniary gain to the debtor from defeasance takes the form of reducing the principal of the debt rather than saving interest, and this benefit accrues only 20 years in the future.

UNCOLLATERALIZED EXIT BONDS

Countries that do not have spare reserves to use in buybacks or as collateral will have to rely on exit bonds and/or debt/equity swaps to secure voluntary debt relief. Uncollateralized exit bonds will certainly require some form of credit enhancement—either guarantees or convincing seniority—if they are to be accepted by banks on terms that confer any worthwhile degree of debt relief. Very few banks will be prepared to accept a major reduction in the present value of their claims unless they believe themselves to be getting a markedly more secure asset in return. The minimal response to the offer of exit bonds on the 1987 Argentine menu was to be expected.

Unfortunately, however, it is very difficult for a country to make a credible unilateral commitment to seniority, for two mutually reinforcing reasons. First, the *pari passu* clause in existing loan contracts forbids the legal subordination of those loans to new instruments, and a waiver of that clause requires *unanimity* on the part of the banks. It seems highly unlikely that each of the hundreds of creditor banks could be persuaded to agree to such a waiver, since each bank correctly perceives such a waiver to weaken its position vis-à-vis other creditors.[16] Hence any seniority has to be de facto (as in the seniority granted to bonds and World Bank loans) rather than de jure. The second difficulty is that it is precisely such informal promises that may sound unconvincing to a creditor when they are advanced in a manner that does not seem to accord with the natural interest of the debtor. And the purchasers of exit bonds, by declaring their desire to cut their ties with the debtor, are clearly not the creditors whose future goodwill a debtor can be expected to go out of its way to nurture.

One might therefore wonder whether it would be possible to establish seniority by introducing as an intermediary some international institution that already enjoys de facto seniority, such as the World Bank. If the World Bank accepted responsibility for collecting the debt-service payments on exit bonds, and then distributed its receipts to creditor banks, could it extend de facto seniority to the exit bonds without placing its own capital at risk? It seems that this is unlikely. Action as a mere agent would probably not suffice to establish credible seniority, which is based on the implicit consent of all

16. Froot (1988) shows that an exception could arise if *every* bank were convinced that a country was over the top of the debt relief Laffer curve, but unanimity on this point seems distinctly improbable.

other creditors. On the other hand, if the Bank became the lender of record or allowed exit bonds to be shaped as B-loans in a cofinancing arrangement, creditor banks would have a claim against the World Bank in the event that debt service was not maintained on schedule. Thus if the Bank is to be involved in the issue of exit bonds it might as well involve itself in an obvious and straightforward way, and use its guarantee authority explicitly.

DEBT/EQUITY SWAPS

Consider finally the option of converting a loan into local currency for equity investment. Even when the country purchases its debt back at less than 100 cents on the dollar, a debt/equity swap is not necessarily a good bargain for the debtor. If the investment would have been made anyway, the country ends up repaying debt prematurely rather than enjoying an inflow of free foreign exchange. So far as the country is concerned, the decisive issues in appraising the desirability of a debt/equity swap can be summarized (Roberts and Remolona 1987) as:

- the proportion of the secondary market discount that the country can succeed in commanding

- the degree of additionality in the direct investment that occurs

- the economic value of the additional investment attracted (e.g., whether it generates foreign exchange or uses abundant resources)

- the pressure on the money supply or, more fundamentally, on real resources caused by the issue of additional currency (a pressure that is absent when the funds flow into newly privatized assets).

Debt/equity swaps were initially envisaged primarily as a mechanism for encouraging direct investment. This led to an assumption that the debtor country should seek to capture only a part of the secondary market discount, leaving the rest as an investment incentive. It also led naturally to concerns about additionality and the economic value of the resulting investment, since one does not wish to subsidize investments that would happen anyway, nor those that neither absorb abundant factors nor generate foreign exchange. However, unless a government has considerable confidence that it can identify particularly worthwhile investments *ex ante*, it may be more sensible to treat debt/equity swaps simply as buybacks in exchange for local currency (with adequate assurance that the investment will stay in local currency, provided by the restrictions on remittance rights). This viewpoint suggests first determining the level of foreign investment that the economy can absorb comfortably, and then auctioning off that amount of local currency in exchange for debt. This will ensure that most of the secondary market discount is captured by the debtor country.

Essentially the same outcome could be achieved by allowing direct investment to enter in the conventional way at the market exchange rate and then using the proceeds for buybacks, assuming that this were allowed. To the debtor country, this procedure would have the advantage of retaining flexibility as to whether to use the proceeds in buybacks rather than in expanding imports. A debt/equity program thus makes sense only (1) if the country is not allowed to buy back its debt; (2) if the inflow of foreign exchange from direct investment would otherwise be preempted for debt service; or (3) if the country wants to subsidize at least some forms of inward direct investment.

5 *The Design of Voluntary Debt Relief*

If all parties have a strong common interest in the facilitation of voluntary debt relief, how can one explain the minuscule scale on which voluntary debt-relief mechanisms have been implemented to date? Four possible reasons come to mind.

The first may be called "catch 22." If a country has the money to buy back a significant volume of debt on the secondary market, then it must also be able to service its debt. But so long as it is servicing its debt, one might expect that the discount at which its loans would trade on the secondary market would be too modest to offer worthwhile debt relief through buybacks.

In fact, Mexican debt has recently traded at a discount as high as 50 percent, despite Mexico having serviced its debt faithfully since 1983 and despite the substantial volume of reserves that Mexico has built up, a part of which could be used for buybacks or other mechanisms that provide debt relief. Presumably this paradox can be explained by concerns that Mexico may not continue to service its debt as punctiliously in the future as it has since 1983 (a concern fostered by, among other things, some statements of President-elect Carlos Salinas de Gortari). Venezuelan debt has also traded at a substantial discount (around 45 percent) despite continued payment of interest, net amortization of over $5 billion during the 1983–87 period, and substantial reserve holdings. These examples suggest that the catch 22 may not be absolute.

A second possible reason is past underestimation of the likely persistence of the debt problem. When the debt crisis first broke, fears for the stability of the international banking system were combined with hopes that the debtor countries might be able to regain voluntary access to capital markets relatively quickly provided that their immediate liquidity problems were contained. This made it rational for banks to reschedule and provide new money, but not to accede to proposals for more fundamental changes like capitalization of a part of interest. As long as banks retained the hope of a relatively rapid normalization of relations with sovereign debtors, the liquidity relief that they regarded themselves as providing was limited. This in turn meant that most banks were reluctant to provide much in the way of debt relief.

A third possible reason for the past lack of voluntary debt relief may have been the perception of a free-rider problem. Cline (1984, 75) provided the definitive analysis of how any bank sufficiently small to believe that its individual action will have no influence on the probability of default has an incentive to avoid new lending (and indeed rescheduling, although that is usually more difficult). If many banks act on their perceptions of individual self-interest, however, it will prove impossible to mobilize the funds that are needed to permit debtors to maintain interest payments. Prevention of free riding has required the dragooning of all banks into the extension of new loans. Any opting out was regarded as a threat to the cohesion of the bank syndicate.

The fourth possible reason concerns the danger of moral hazard, which arises with schemes for voluntary as well as comprehensive debt relief. Debtor countries would still have an incentive to cast doubt on their continued ability or willingness to service debt, so as to reduce the price at which they could buy back their debt on the secondary market or enhance the attractiveness of other instruments that confer debt relief.

It seems to be widely believed that these considerations preclude a major role for voluntary debt relief in the resolution of the debt crisis. It is often conceded that mechanisms like debt/equity swaps or buybacks may have a useful role at the margin, but nothing more. In fact, the four possible explanations for the modest scale of voluntary debt relief in the past do not necessarily imply that its future role need remain so circumscribed. It has already been pointed out that catch 22 looks more conclusive in theory than it seems to be in practice. Second, most banks have by now recognized that the problem is an enduring one and that they cannot realistically anticipate a return to voluntary lending in the foreseeable future. Third, the free-rider charge is inapplicable provided that creditors who exit do so at a price, by providing debt relief. Moral hazard remains a key issue, but it is one that it may be possible to address through the appropriate design of proposals.

FACILITATING BUYBACKS

The changes that need to be made in order to promote buybacks are the removal of legal obstacles and the provision of sufficient financial leeway to allow countries to exploit their new legal freedom.

It is not altogether clear whether buybacks are presently precluded by the mandatory prepayment clause in loan contracts, which requires that any prepayment must be done "ratably" (i.e., that all banks must be repaid proportionately to their exposure), or by the sharing clause, which requires banks to share proportionately any disproportionate payments they receive. In the case of Bolivia, the banks agreed to waive these clauses so as to remove any doubts. Other countries that have made modest buybacks of public or publicly guaranteed loans are believed to have done so by using state agencies other than the original borrower as the purchaser, with a view to avoiding any possible challenge. In any event, the present situation is sufficiently ambiguous to make it desirable for the banks to be asked to provide waivers as a means of facilitating buybacks, as they are reportedly planning to do with Chile.

Suspension of the mandatory prepayment and sharing clauses requires the consent of all the creditor banks, but their approval in response to a recommendation from the Bank Advisory Committee may nonetheless be expected since individual banks do not perceive themselves to be worsening their position vis-à-vis other creditors. The Committee might make an annual recommendation in favor of such a waiver, perhaps up to a specified limit, whenever a debtor country was judged to be servicing its debt conscientiously. This would provide an incentive for the debtor to avoid actions that might reduce the value of its debt, thus providing at least a partial solution to the problem of moral hazard. It would also give the banks a way to reward responsible behavior.

The other prerequisite for buybacks is the availability of reserves. Even if the banks accept that discounted buybacks are in the interest of those banks that remain as well as that of the debtor and the exiting banks, they may find it difficult to agree to new money packages that explicitly provide cash for the debtor to finance buybacks. Banks are bound to be concerned about the propriety of lending new money that they will show in their balance sheets at face value if that money is used to enable the debtor to buy back old debt at a fraction of that value. A possible solution to this problem would be to earmark certain revenue streams for use in buybacks. From the banks' perspective, the ideal would be to avoid any diversion of income from debt service to buybacks. The earmarked streams should thus consist of revenues that would not otherwise have been available—like the use of funds specifically donated by sympathetic governments for the purpose of financing buybacks, as occurred in Bolivia.

Since donor governments are unlikely to donate earmarked aid for buybacks, except in a situation as extreme as that of Bolivia, it will probably be necessary for the banks to accept some compromise with their ideal and accept the earmarking of revenues which might have been available in any event. It would still be sensible to seek revenue streams that are particularly sensitive to policy actions by the debtor country, for incentive reasons. Promising candidates would be the repatriation of flight capital, inward direct investment, and a proportion of the increase in revenues from nontraditional exports.

The earmarking of specified revenue streams as legitimate sources of finance for buybacks does not seem to confront any legal problem, since the country would not be pledging itself to use particular revenues or assets for buybacks. The earmarking would be accomplished by the earmarked revenues being disregarded in the negotiations between a debtor and its Bank Advisory Committee regarding the necessary scale of new lending.

LAUNCHING EXIT BONDS

It was argued in section 4 that successful issue of exit bonds will require either collateralization, guarantees, or convincing seniority. Collateralized exit bonds seem rather pointless, since the reserves they require can be used as or more efficiently in a buyback program.[17] Seniority is impractical because a waiver of the nonsubordination clause requires the unanimous consent of the lending banks. The most promising possibility thus involves guarantees.

The central question concerns who would provide the guarantees. The obvious candidate is the World Bank. The Bank was given the legal authority to issue guarantees in its original Articles, though it has never used those powers on an extensive scale.[18] It has just received a general capital increase of $75 billion, giving it ample financial scope to launch a substantial guarantee program rapidly. It has the capacity and experience to impose some form of conditionality, which will surely be needed: no guarantor can sensibly provide guarantees without assurance that the debtor's policies will be such as to enable it to service its debts and avoid the guarantees being called. Finally, the Bank has a legal mechanism whereby it can give the exit bonds the de facto seniority that would provide the primary safeguard against the guarantee being called; that is, it can require a counter-guarantee from the debtor government and can insert an optional cross-default clause between that counter-guarantee and the rest of its loans.

Other features of Bank-guaranteed exit bonds are suggested below. Clearly many of the details could be varied, but it seems useful to lay out a specific set of proposals in order to illuminate the issues that will need to be resolved and demonstrate that reasonable solutions can be devised.

The exit instruments would presumably take the form of securitized bonds to facilitate their transferability. However, this does not seem a topic of decisive importance: a special loan issue could be substituted.

---

17. Press reports at the time of the Toronto Summit (June 1988) suggested that Japan had presented a proposal along these lines, which envisaged that a debtor nation agreeing to a structural adjustment program with the IMF should have the right to issue exit bonds corresponding to a part of its debt and should partially collateralize those bonds with a reserve account established at the IMF. Since the debtor country would be responsible for establishing the reserve account out of its own reserves (apparently with no input from either Japan or the IMF), this proposal is vulnerable to the same criticism of cost-ineffective use of foreign exchange as the Mexican defeasance scheme.

18. There has been some legal question concerning whether guarantees that provide debt relief rather than induce new money are consistent with the requirement in the Bank's Articles that loans be made only for "productive purposes." The economics of the matter seem clear enough: debt relief can indeed be expected to increase the level of productive investment in a country that is constrained by a shortage of foreign exchange. With the proper political lead the lawyers could doubtless be persuaded to adopt a legal interpretation consistent with economic reality.

The World Bank should not be expected to tie up a large part of its capital indefinitely in guaranteeing exit bonds. On the contrary, this should be a crash program that might absorb a large part of the leeway provided by the recent general capital increase over the next few years but would be phased out relatively quickly in order to release the Bank's resources for its conventional lending programs as these build up. One should therefore avoid a balloon repayment of principal at the end, which would impose a big contingent liability on the Bank for the full life of the exit bonds. The debt service on exit bonds should instead take the form of a series of equal payments covering both interest and principal (as in a mortgage).

The same consideration points to a relatively short maturity, at least for the guaranteed portion of the loan. This is also consistent with the need for some form of conditionality (a topic discussed further below), since not even the most fervent advocates of conditionality believe that this can provide any assurance of prudent policies for more than a few years in the future. The corresponding disadvantage is that it will provide little or no cash-flow relief to the debtor in the short run, which implies that any additional cash-flow relief will have to be provided by the banks that choose not to exit. These banks will have to realize that, at least under unfavorable contingencies for the country, they are bound to suffer a reduced cash flow in the short run. The attraction of an exit bond—for which the exiting banks are prepared to concede a fall in present value that will ultimately redound in part to the benefit of the banks that do not exit—is that it bestows seniority.

Suppose that the payment coupon on the exit bonds were set equal to the interest coupon on regular bank loans. If swapped at face value, this would leave a debtor's payments obligation unchanged: the purchasers of exit bonds would not provide cash-flow relief, while the nonexiting banks would be penalized (via a smaller base for new money requirements or higher interest capitalization) only to the extent that the country was unable to meet its full interest bill or as a result of a decision that more cash-flow relief was needed. The maturity of the World Bank's guarantee might be chosen so as to make the present value of the exit bond for a typical debtor roughly equal to the price on the secondary market, since this would then result in exit bonds and loans typically being swapped close to par (thus leaving debtors' payments obligations unchanged). With current interest rates (LIBOR + spread) of around 9 percent and secondary market prices of 50 cents on the dollar, this criterion implies a maturity of 8 years.[19]

19. $\sum_{t=1}^{8} 9/(1.09)^t = 49.8.$

The maturity of the Bank's guarantee need not necessarily be the same as the maturity of the exit bond. In fact, there is a strong incentive argument for structuring the exit bonds to provide for additional payments in the event that they suffer any payments interruption. For example, the bonds could initially be issued with 16-year maturities, with the first eight payments guaranteed by the World Bank and the remaining eight subject to cancellation, one year at a time, as the first eight were paid off on schedule. The resulting incentive for the debtor to maintain the service of these bonds would further reduce the probability that the Bank's guarantees would ever be called.

Suppose, therefore, that exit bonds promise to pay a fixed sum[20] to their purchasers each year for eight years (with the possibility of further payments if the eight guaranteed payments are not made on time). The process of issuing those bonds could be organized in two ways. One would be to fix the annual coupon payment on the exit bond and the price at which existing bank credits could be swapped into exit bonds, and issue the quantity of exit bonds that the banks want to take up at those prices. The alternative is to fix the annual coupon payment on the exit bond and the (maximum) number of bonds to be issued, and allow the banks to bid for the exit bonds. As with the Mexican defeasance scheme, those banks willing to bid attractively low prices at which they would swap their existing loans would have their bids accepted.

The second approach seems much more attractive. It avoids the need to guess prices that will entice the banks to exit. It does not give any official recognition to the secondary market price. (The banks themselves will doubtless take account of that price, since that is the main alternative mechanism for exit, but that does not raise similar problems.) Finally, by forcing the banks to compete for a limited volume of guarantees, it avoids any suggestion that public money is being used to bail out the banks.

In order to ensure that the World Bank used its guarantee authority only to purchase substantial debt relief, it should stipulate a maximum swap price at which its guarantee would apply. A requirement that debt relief be at least 35 percent might be reasonable. This would allow all the highly indebted countries a chance to issue exit bonds without requiring a further fall in prices on the secondary market, while ensuring that World Bank guarantees were not frittered away without purchasing a worthwhile degree of debt relief.

20. Alternatively, by analogy with a variable-rate mortgage, the sum due could vary each year by reference to the current level of LIBOR. Better still, it could vary with respect to an index of ability to pay, such as export revenue or export prices.

The Bank would also have to determine a maximum value for exit bonds that it was prepared to guarantee for any individual country. It seems pointless to try and invent any formula to guide this decision. Overall, if one estimates that perhaps one-third of the debt is held by banks that would be willing to sell out for a substantial discount (averaging 50 percent), the potential demand from the 17 highly indebted countries could amount to as much as $45 billion. A sum as large as this would strain the Bank's financial capacity under present plans, but any conflict with the lending program could be avoided by accelerating subscription of the $75 billion general capital increase already agreed.

In practice, the Bank should probably be guided by two factors in the decision as to how many exit bonds to guarantee. One factor is how much debt relief it is likely to be able to buy, for which it can get a clue from the price on the secondary market. The other is how confident it can be that the country will indeed service its exit bonds on schedule and not trigger the Bank's guarantee, which it will have to judge by the quality of the country's economic policies. It would be irresponsible, indeed dangerous, for the Bank to start guaranteeing debts above the level that it is confident a country will be able and willing to service.

This inevitably means that the Bank's guarantees will involve conditionality. The question is what form that conditionality should take. My own view is that it makes sense to concentrate on a limited number of strategic factors that ensure that no new disaster is in the making (and to involve the IMF as well as the Bank in judging whether policy is sustainable). Far better that the Bank should insist on an assurance that debtors are implementing a responsible fiscal strategy and maintaining a competitive exchange rate than that it buy more promises that trade restrictions will be dismantled or state enterprises privatized. In addition to reinforcing elementary prudence, perhaps the Bank should pursue the idea of a "debt-for-nature" bargain urged by environmental groups. The creditors whose guarantees are being used do, after all, have a material interest in limiting the greenhouse effect and species extinction and thus in curbing the destruction of tropical forests.

Having developed a proposal, it is natural to try to anticipate some of the arguments that might be developed in criticism. First, the Bank has customarily sought to avoid using its guarantee authority because of the potential conflict with its lending program, which it regards as its primary activity. (Guarantees count dollar-for-dollar against the Bank's callable capital, just like loans; they differ, however, in that they impose no requirement to raise cash from the private market.) The answer is that a temporary program of guaranteeing exit bonds need not obstruct the regular lending program. Assuming an average discount of 50 percent, conversion of $90 billion (one-third of the bank debt of the seventeen highly indebted countries or about 23 percent of the banks' total LDC debt) into guaranteed exit bonds with an eight-year maturity in a four-year program would impose a maximum claim against the Bank's capital of $37 billion at the end of the fourth year (declining to $31 billion after 5 years and zero after 12 years.) If subscriptions under the general capital increase are paid in on an accelerated schedule, commitments on that scale would not constrain the Bank's lending program until long after the new sustainable lending level of $22 billion had been reached, if ever.

Second, it will doubtless be claimed that a decision to use the Bank's guarantee authority would jeopardize the chance that the US Congress will ratify the US contribution to the general capital increase (which has still not been approved as this goes to press, though enough other countries have ratified for the increase to take effect). In fact, however, the complaint of some congressional critics has been that the World Bank was not playing any role in resolving the debt crisis by catalyzing debt relief from the banks. Exit bonds would do exactly that—admittedly not on the comprehensive basis that the congressional critics have envisaged, but no less effectively. A program of World Bank guarantees for exit bonds thus ought to help secure, rather than jeopardize, congressional ratification of the general capital increase.

Third, it may be suggested that there exist more suitable guarantors than the World Bank. For example, Shafiqul Islam (1988) has argued for a reconstruction of bank claims into long-term bonds with concessional interest rates that would be guaranteed by the main surplus countries, Japan and West Germany, rather than by the World Bank. However, a current account surplus is an irrelevant criterion for selecting a guarantor: a credible guarantee requires positive net worth, not a positive flow of funds. The World Bank's capital is distributed roughly in proportion to countries' financial strength, and is thus a more suitable base against which to match the role of guarantor. Moreover, the Bank has the experience to impose conditionality and a continuing relationship with the debtors that should provide assurance that the exit bonds will be treated as senior.

Fourth, parts of the Bank's bureaucracy will fret about the danger that its creditworthiness will be eroded and its cost of borrowing will rise. This may conceivably occur, but on a very limited scale. The impact can hardly be large, since the ultimate security of those who lend to the Bank is provided by the callable capital contributed by the industrial countries rather than the quality of the Bank's loan (or guarantee) portfolio. A modest service charge could easily ensure that the Bank's other clients benefit financially, rather than being penalized, by its role in guaranteeing exit bonds. The Bank needs to worry more about furthering the purposes for which it was founded and less about achieving results that impress the graduates of finance schools.

A POSSIBLE SUPPLEMENT TO VOLUNTARY APPROACHES

Calculations made in the next section suggest that the voluntary measures discussed above—buybacks and exit bonds—should suffice to bring significant relief to the cash-flow position of all except the most hopelessly indebted countries eventually. Unfortunately, that relief will be about a decade in coming, so a more rapid resolution of the debt crisis will remain dependent on export growth. One can of course hope that stabilization of the debtors' financial prospects would ease the process of raising new money, encourage the repatriation of flight capital, and improve the prospects for other forms of capital inflow. Nevertheless, it is prudent to give some consideration to measures that might supplement the voluntary approach, should the need arise.

That need could arise for several reasons. The world economic environment might change for the worse. The process of assembling new money packages might finally collapse, as has repeatedly been feared. Voluntarism may prove insufficient for countries in a particularly difficult situation. The political climate could change, leading to a commitment to achieve rapidly a definitive solution to the debt crisis.

What would be desirable is a mechanism that would face the banks with an unambiguous choice between greater security and faster repayment at the cost of a reduction in present value, on the one hand, and maintenance of the present value of contractual claims at the cost of a delay in repayment, on the other. The key to this would be a reconstruction of the debt of the nonexiting banks on terms that the debtor countries could reasonably be expected to live with under a wide range of circumstances. Such a reconstruction would need to provide adequate liquidity relief even if payments outcomes turned out worse than hoped. This would provide a solution to the problem of debtor moral hazard, since access to voluntary debt relief could be made conditional on the debt continuing to be serviced in accordance with the new commitments. Note also that confidence of full future debt-service payments need not preclude volunteers from providing debt relief once the possibility of free riding is suppressed and it is unambiguously established that banks that do not give debt relief can expect to wait a long time to get their money back.

Such a definitive debt reconstruction would clearly require the consent of the bulk of the banks, acting through the Bank Advisory Committee. This consent is unlikely to be forthcoming unless the banks believe that the debt reconstruction will leave them at least as well off as they could expect to be under existing arrangements. In principle it should be possible to meet this requirement, given the two potential sources of gain to the nonexiting banks analyzed in section 3: the incentive effect of debt relief (the debt relief Laffer curve) and the income transfer from the banks that choose to exit. But the banks will have to recognize that their cash flow is likely to be squeezed for some years, until the exit bonds have been paid off, since it is the nonexiting banks that will be expected to provide cash-flow relief in the short run.

If the net interest (after receipt of new money or interest capitalization) that a country is expected to pay is to vary so as to provide adequate liquidity relief under a wide range of circumstances without the need for negotiation, it will be necessary to agree on a formula to govern the payments obligation. The simplest candidate is a formula linking payments obligations to the value of export receipts. This has the virtue both of ensuring that the creditors benefit from improved export performance and of protecting the debtors from a deterioration in the world environment. The way to reconcile a payments obligation linked to payments capacity with maintenance of the present value of the contractual claims of the creditors is to capitalize any excess of interest charges over the payments obligation. If some or all banks prefer to retain the form of new money packages, presumably they could devise a corresponding formula for their new money obligation.

One specific way to implement this approach would be to specify the debt-service *payments* due in any future year as an agreed sum that the country was capable of servicing on the basis of its export performance in some base year, plus some proportion of *incremental* export revenue[21] over the value

21. Provided that adequate statistics are available, it would seem logical to include revenue from exports of goods, services, and transfers. In principle, a case can be made for tying debt-service charges to variables that have an important influence on export revenue but that are entirely exogenous to the country involved, such as the prices of important primary commodity exports, so as to avoid the disincentive effect of tying debt service to exports. However, the practical problems of devising a measure that can be relied upon to track aggregate ability to pay suggest that such an approach would be difficult to employ in comprehensive debt reconstruction (as opposed to future voluntary lending or restructuring of individual claims: see Lessard and Williamson 1985).

in the base year. (If export revenue falls below that of the base year, presumably the debt-service payment might also fall.) This bears a resemblance to proposals to limit debt-service payments to a proportion of exports (option 17 in Bergsten, Cline, and Williamson 1985), but it is more flexible in that the proportion of *additional* export revenue to be devoted to debt service can be set higher than that in the base year. This should help to reconcile the need of the debtors for significant cash-flow relief as long as circumstances remain bad with the creditors' desire to have a substantial stake in any future upturn in the debtors' fortunes. It also bears a resemblance to the limit on debt service to 10 percent of export value decreed by President Alan Garcia of Peru, but differs in the additional and fundamental sense that it is a proposal for mutually agreed debt reconstruction rather than for unilateral action.[22]

It is the essence of this proposal that debt-service *charges* would be distinct from current payments obligations. Charges would continue to be based on the value of debt outstanding. Both interest and amortization could continue to be assessed in essentially the same way as at present. But any excess of interest charges over debt-service payments due would be capitalized. Similarly, all maturing debt would be automatically rolled over except when debt-service payments exceeded the interest charge.[23]

---

22. The proposal is (almost) a combination of option 16 (interest capitalization instead of new money) and option 17 (payments based on exports) considered in Bergsten, Cline, and Williamson (1985). At that time we did not recommend adoption of such options, which we argued would delay the return of debtor countries to normal access to capital markets, but instead treated them as contingency plans for possible utilization in the event of a deterioration in the debt situation. Unfortunately, there is no sign of a restoration of normal market access for most debtor countries. Meanwhile the ability of the banks to accommodate solutions that involve reductions in reported earnings has improved, while evidence has increasingly suggested that reported earnings are of much less significance than previously assumed. It is these developments that justify considering the use of some of the contingency measures that were previously deemed undesirable.

23. These ideas are easily expressed in algebra. Debt service payments due in year t, P_t, would be

$$P_t = \alpha + \beta (X_{t-1} - X_o)$$

where α is the sum the country was capable of servicing in the base year, β is the percentage of incremental export revenue to be devoted to debt service, and X_o is the value of export revenue in the base year. Debt service charges, C_t, would be

$$C_t = (i + a) D_t$$

where i is the interest rate, a is the amortization rate, and D is the outstanding value of debt. The value of the debt would change according to the formula

$$D_{t+1} - D_t = iD_t - P_t.$$

The aim would then be to select the crucial parameters—the debt service that the country was capable of handling in the base year and the proportion of its incremental export receipts to be applied to servicing debt—so as to leave the debtor with an adequate short-run cash flow and the nonexiting banks at least as well-off in the long run as they could expect to be under present arrangements and with present export prospects. To the extent that export prospects improve because of better incentives facing the debtor country, the banks can expect to benefit eventually. To the extent that some loans are bought back cheaply on the secondary market, more debt service will ultimately be available for the banks that remain. To the extent that some banks buy exit bonds, the remaining banks will have to capitalize a higher proportion of interest in the short run, but this will be compensated by the greater interest receipts they can expect in the long run after the exit bonds are paid off. (Banks that are not compensated by the expectation of greater long-run interest receipts will be the ones that choose to exit.)

Provided that some banks are sufficiently impatient or pessimistic about the prospects of debtors as to be willing to exit for prices below the present value of expected debt service, the banks that remain can expect to receive a stream of earnings with a higher expected present value as a result of capitalization plus the facilitation of voluntary debt relief. However, the expected present value of future earnings is not necessarily the primary concern of accountants and regulators.

The accounting and regulatory implications of interest capitalization and of payments linked to exports were evaluated in Bergsten, Cline, and Williamson (1985, 157–58, 168). It was concluded that in both cases the American accounting profession would be likely to take a view that would result in a reduction in the reported value of bank profits. In the case of a combined scheme, it would seem highly unlikely that the accountants would allow accrual into profits of that portion of interest charges in excess of interest receipts.

This is not, however, a decisive argument against the proposal. There is now overwhelming evidence that the level of reported bank profits is not a critical determinant of the stock market valuation of bank shares. The stock market saw through the attempt of the banks (encouraged by officials) to pretend that the value of their sovereign loans had been unimpaired by the debt crisis. The market can perhaps be expected to value the increase in bank claims resulting from capitalization about as highly (or lowly) as that resulting from involuntary lending, even if the accountants continue to insist that the former process does not generate income that can be accrued into profits and the latter does. Furthermore, banks that wished to preserve the legal fiction that interest was not being capitalized could be allowed to place an equivalent amount of "new money" in an escrow account from which a part of their interest payments would be drawn. A procedure like this was employed in the Polish restructuring in 1981.

It is less likely that a definitive debt reconstruction would be classified as a "troubled debt restructuring" (which occurs when the accountants judge that a restructuring involves a "concession") than it would have been if such changes had been made piecemeal in a series of emergency responses to the debt crisis. One can indeed argue that automatic interest capitalization in excess of a formula related to export earnings would have provided a more logical basis for medium-term sovereign loans than the floating interest rates that were incorporated in past loans.

Finally, it is the regulators rather than the accountants who decide whether loans have to be classified as "value-impaired," which carries the penalty of having to reserve a specified percentage against the loans involved. In making such decisions, the regulators need to consider the health of the banking system. Once they concluded that innovations in bank practice presented the best chance of preserving the present value of bank claims, it would be counterproductive to classify loans that implemented those innovations as value-impaired.

None of this is to suggest that the accountants, the bankers, or the stock market would be likely to welcome the capitalization of interest in excess of a ceiling based on the value of exports. What it does suggest is that their anguish would be no greater than that of the banks that decide to sacrifice present value and grant debt relief, or of the debtors. No one is likely to be particularly happy with a definitive debt reconstruction, which of necessity involves definitive recognition of past mistakes. The question is whether a better alternative exists.

Another possible objection to definitive debt reconstruction is that it might weaken the pressures for policy reform by the debtors. The requirement of negotiating new money packages gives the banks leverage to insist that the debtor implement what they perceive to be appropriate policies. The banks generally exercise this leverage by requiring that the debtor negotiate a high-conditionality program with the IMF. Once debt-service obligations had been cut back to a level that the country could handle, it would lose this close foreign monitoring of its economy.

This might be a strong objection if there were convincing evidence that effective conditionality programs could be designed and monitored over lengthy periods. In fact, however, the evidence seems distinctly discouraging (see Sachs 1988 for a recent appraisal). Indeed, the Fund itself has never exhibited much confidence in its ability to design and monitor medium-run (let alone long-run) programs. It seems sensible enough to require that the banks be satisfied with the thrust of policy at the time when the definitive debt reconstruction is negotiated, and the best mechanisms available for judging the adequacy of policy remain IMF conditionality and World Bank structural adjustment lending. It was also suggested above that the Bank might make access to exit bonds conditional upon prudent fiscal and exchange rate policies. But the purpose of a definitive debt reconstruction is to permit a return to normality, and endless high-conditionality IMF programs are not, and should not be considered, normal for any country.

A standard argument against capping interest payments and interest capitalization has been that debtor countries would prejudice their own futures if they participated, by jeopardizing their future access to bank lending. Unfortunately, the debt crisis has already lingered so long that this argument has lost much of its force: most debtor countries already seem condemned to at best limited access to the international capital market for some years.

It has even been counterargued that historical experience shows little evidence of countries suffering future loss of access to credit markets as a result of default; on the contrary, a reduction in outstanding debt is asserted to create favorable conditions for a resumption of lending (Kaletsky 1985; Jorgensen and Sachs 1988). However convincing the evidence from the past, it would be rash to extrapolate this sort of empirical regularity into the future.

The most prudent course would seem to be one that avoids both unlimited current sacrifices in the hope of restoring access to bank credit and casual disregard of the interests of creditors. One has to doubt whether a debt reconstruction that avoids prejudicing lenders relative to what they can currently expect, and that permits debtors to recover faster than currently seems likely, can really be bad for the debtors' future creditworthiness.

Another possible argument against automatic capitalization in excess of a cap determined by export earnings is that under particularly adverse circumstances—namely a long period of unexpectedly low export earnings—a country's total external debt could compound to an unmanageably large sum. However, it is important to remember that this proposal is being advanced in conjunction with the facilitation of buybacks. As a country's debt mounted, its price on the secondary market would decline. The debtor would be entitled to use some if its export earnings to buy back debt at this low price, thereby tending to offset the increase in debt resulting from interest capitalization. Thus even in this worst-case scenario, the two proposals together (formula-determined interest capitalization and buybacks) would lead to a self-equilibrating system, which is surely an advantage over present arrangements.

The definitive debt reconstruction envisaged here would need to be negotiated in the same way as the many reschedulings already agreed, with discussions between the authorities of each individual debtor country and the Bank Advisory Committee, followed by acceptance of the terms by each of the country's commercial bank creditors that did not choose to exit. The new loans could presumably carry standard interest rates. They would be of indeterminate duration, specifying a rate of amortization following any grace period. They would also provide for a rollover of principal as well as capitalization of interest whenever debt-service charges exceeded payments due as calculated by the formula related to the level of export receipts. The parties would have to agree on a mechanism for verifying the value of exports to be used in the formula. Clearly these proposals involve some substantial innovations in current banking practices, even though they are intended to do no more than formalize what actually happens now. The legitimate interest of the banks would be to ensure that the new arrangements did not leave them worse off than they could have expected to be under current practices.

The principal problem, as always in rescheduling, would be to deal with the fringe of banks not prepared to accept these terms. The best solution would be to let them hold on to their existing loans (and keep open the option of conversion to the new terms) indefinitely, while cutting back interest payments to the level that would have applied had they accepted the offer of conversion. The banks involved would then presumably accumulate arrears, which would have the same result as the interest capitalization involved in the new terms. The nonconverting banks would be unable to use the sharing clause to sue the banks that did convert since the payments made to both groups of banks would be proportionate. Hence the only legal redress of the nonconverting banks would be to sue the debtor and seek to seize its assets—the doomsday weapon that the banks have always shrunk from using up to now. It hardly seems likely that a fringe bank would incur the legal costs, the risks, and the odium of wielding the doomsday weapon when the option of exit was simultaneously being facilitated.

6 *The Potential of Voluntary Debt Relief*

It is increasingly widely accepted that resolution of the debt crisis will require a measure of debt relief. Indeed, the Toronto Summit in June 1988 approved a framework agreement for the provision of relief on official debt to the poorest heavily indebted countries, primarily in sub-Saharan Africa. Although the summit leaders did not bring themselves to endorse any comparable initiative for the middle-income debtors or commercial bank loans, their endorsement of "innovative financing techniques . . . that . . . are voluntary, market oriented and applied on a case by case basis" (Summit Communiqué, paragraph 27) suggests their openness to much of the approach developed in this study.

Some economists argue that the middle-income debtors are already getting substantial debt relief. For example, Bulow and Rogoff (1988) treat new money agreements as partial default rather than postponement of interest. Their premise is that the debt is too large for there to be a significant chance that it will ever be fully serviced without new money, and that creditors and debtors are engaged in essentially continuous and permanent negotiations as to what fraction of their obligations the debtors can afford to pay. This view implies that any repurchase of marginal debt is of minimal significance or benefit to the debtor: since it has to be repurchased at a price that reflects the average expected interest payments, the cost of repurchase exceeds the benefit. The policy conclusion is that the debtors are already getting debt relief and should learn to appreciate their good fortune.

The view underlying the present study is quite different. I accept that many bank creditors, holding perhaps as much as one-third of LDC debt, share the pessimistic Bulow–Rogoff view (or are prepared to act as though they did for various institutional reasons, which may include a belief that their stockholders share that view). But I believe that view is wrong (for reasons laid out most fully by Cohen 1985). If they find the short and medium run tolerable, debtors will be capable of servicing their debt fully in the long run. One way of making the medium run shorter, and thus more tolerable, is to exploit the pessimistic creditors who share the Bulow–Rogoff view, which one can do either by buying back their debt or selling them guaranteed exit bonds at prices that reflect their pessimistic expectations. Since given their expectations they will feel it is they that are doing the exploiting, everyone will be happy, or at least less unhappy.

Hence the first step is to facilitate buybacks, by having the banks periodically agree to waive the sharing clause. Such a gesture would not amount to much unless countries have some source of cash with which they can finance buybacks when they judge purchase worthwhile. It was suggested in section 4 that this might be accomplished by agreeing that certain revenue streams would be disregarded when the banks negotiate new money packages. The next step is to have the World Bank inaugurate an immediate program to guarantee exit bonds issued by debtor countries whose policies merit confidence that the guarantees will not be called.

How much could voluntary debt relief accomplish? The data and calculations in the tables are intended to give a rough answer. Table 1 shows certain cash flows for the 17 highly indebted middle-income countries from 1983 to 1988. The figures for 1988 are not actual outcomes or even forecasts of probable

TABLE 1 **Cash flows of the 17 highly indebted countries, 1983–88** (billion dollars)

	1983	*1984*	*1985*	*1986*	*1987*	*1988*[a]
Exports of goods and services	138.1	153.7	149.1	132.3	n.a.	150
Interest payments	29.6	34.2	33.6	31.1	32.8	34.0
on long term public debt to banks	17.4	19.2	20.9	18.8	19.3	20.1
other (official, private, IMF,[b] suppliers)	12.2	15.0	12.7	12.3	13.5	13.9
Capital inflows	19.2	10.9	10.0	5.2	n.a.	11.8
from banks, "new money"	13.1	4.6	6.5	0.3	10.3	6.6
other loans	6.1	6.3	3.5	4.9	n.a.	5.2
Negative resource transfer (implied)	10.4	23.3	23.6	25.9	n.a.	22.2
Negative resource transfer (actual)	7.5	17.5	26.1	24.8	20.0	n.a.
Memorandum item: direct investment	3.4	3.2	4.5	2.9	n.a.	3.5

Sources: World Debt Tables, 1987–88 edition, vol. I, pp. 30–33 and Table 2, p. xiii for actual resource transfer. *International Financial Statistics* for direct investment. Institute of International Finance for new bank lending.

n.a. = not available

a. Data for 1988 are plausible trend values.

b. Estimated.

TABLE 2 **Resource transfer under alternative scenarios**

	"1990"		"2000"	
	Billion dollars	*Percentage of exports of goods & services*	*Billion dollars*	*Percentage of exports of goods & services*
No debt relief				
Constant debt	−33.9	20.5	−33.0	12.2
Baker Plan	−23.9	14.5	−32.1	11.9
Buybacks				
Constant debt	−30.6	18.5	−33.0	12.2
Same borrowing as Baker Plan	−26.8	16.2	−25.4	9.4
Exit bonds				
Constant debt	−27.4	16.6	−33.0	12.2
Same borrowing as Baker Plan	−23.9	14.5	−25.4	9.4

Source: Table 1.

outcomes, but rather estimates of plausible "trend" values for 1988. (It is likely, for example, that exports will in the event exceed $150 billion, owing to strong prices of many primary commodities.) The figure for new lending by banks is that implied by the Baker Plan.[24]

The figures for the implied negative resource transfers in table 1 are interest payments *less* borrowing. The main inadequacy of these figures is that they exclude both profit remittances and inflows of direct investment (shown as a memorandum item), but the two tend to cancel. A comparison of the implied transfers and the World Bank's estimates of actual transfers (shown in the following row) indicates that the discrepancies are not so large as to preclude the use of the statistics in the table for projecting resource transfers.

The data in table 1 are used to construct the estimates of negative resource transfers under various scenarios shown in table 2. The year "1990" represents a year when buybacks are in progress or exit bonds are being serviced, while the year "2000" represents a year when cash flows are benefiting from the

24. New money packages agreed with the 17 highly indebted countries in 1986–87 summed to $10.6 billion, somewhat less than the $13.2 billion target increase proposed in the Baker Plan.

completion of buybacks or the payoff of exit bonds. The table compares negative resource transfers in each ''year'' without debt relief in the first panel, and with buybacks and exit bonds in the other two panels. In each of these three cases, the table shows the outcome with two alternative assumptions about the future path of debt: that it is held constant after 1988, and that the country borrows henceforth at the rate provided for by the Baker Plan. This is interpreted as constant annual lending of $6.6 billion by the banks and $5.2 billion by all other lenders. (This results in total debt increasing from an estimated $489 billion in 1988 to $630 billion in 2000, without debt relief.)

The other principal assumptions incorporated in the calculations are:

- that the estimated 1987 interest rates of 7.7 percent on bank debt and 6.1 percent on other loans remain constant at those levels

- that one-third of bank debt could be bought back for an average discount of 50 percent either through buybacks or through exit bonds[25]

- that exit bonds have a maturity of 9.4 years and a coupon of 7.7 per year (and therefore have a present value of 50 percent when discounting at the banks' interest rate), and are all issued in 1989

- that buybacks would occur at a constant rate over the same 9.4 years that exit bonds would be serviced

- that after 1988 exports grow at a constant rate of 5 percent per year. (If one assumes that smaller negative resource transfers in early years were partially devoted to investment in export production, exports would be larger and therefore the ratio of resource transfers to exports smaller in 2000 in the cases where borrowing proceeds according to the Baker Plan.)

Inspection of table 2 suggests a number of conclusions. The first is that a major erosion in the negative resource transfer as a percentage of exports (to a level below that currently implied by the Baker Plan) ultimately can be expected even without debt relief, overwhelmingly as a result of the growth

25. It is more reasonable to assume that such a large volume of exit bonds might be issued at close to the present secondary market price than that an equivalent value of buybacks could be achieved at such a low price, since the price on the secondary market would rise as debt declined while the banks would be required to bid for exit bonds at a time when the debtor's prospects were still clouded. However, the assumption that voluntary debt relief would take place on similar terms under either mechanism is needed to permit a clean comparison.

in exports. It remains true that the best cure for the debt crisis is to grow out of it. It is true that export values failed to grow after 1982 (table 1): the rise in export volumes was offset by weak export prices, especially for primary products. But this unhappy state of affairs should not last indefinitely. As long as investment in export industries is not cut back too severely (as could conceivably happen if the negative resource transfer became excessive), exports can be expected to grow again sooner or later and ease the debt problem even without debt relief.

A second conclusion is that, unless one believes the Baker Plan was wrong to reduce the negative resource transfer, a policy of attempting to prevent any further buildup in debt would be ill-conceived. That remains true even in the presence of debt relief on the scale envisaged here, at least until buybacks are complete or exit bonds are paid off, i.e., until the late 1990s. Despite their current difficulties, these countries are natural capital importers, and the aim of policy should be to increase rather than curtail the capital that flows to them, even at the cost of a further buildup in debt.

Third, it is apparent that the benefits of a buyback program would be positive but quite modest. With a constant long-run level of debt (by assumption), the benefits all accrue in the short run: buybacks on the scale hypothesized would reduce the cost of stabilizing the debt by a little more than $3 billion per year. Under a policy of continuing to borrow on the scale of the Baker Plan, the long-run benefit of buybacks would be quite substantial (a reduction of almost 3 percent in the negative resource transfer as a fraction of exports). But in the short run, buybacks cost cash, and therefore the negative resource transfer as a fraction of exports is almost 3 percent larger than under the Baker Plan. Given the presumption that the foreign exchange shortage should ease over time, this suggests that buybacks might best be used as a way of making profitable use of unexpected foreign-exchange windfalls.

Fourth, it can be seen that exit bonds dominate buybacks. Under a constant-debt objective they lead to the same long-run outcome as the other two strategies (that equality is inherent in maintaining debt constant), but the short-run cost is lower. In particular, exit bonds dominate buybacks in the short run because the entire one-third of the debt that is by assumption being bought back at 50 percent is dealt with up front,[26] whereas under the

26. In practice this might be over three or four years, but this would still lead to a quicker realization of the interest savings than would be possible under buybacks.

alternative strategy the country continues to pay full interest on loans that will ultimately be bought back until it can afford the buyback. This advantage is additional to the greater chance of being able to secure a favorable discount for a large volume of debt through the auction of exit bonds as opposed to relying on buybacks (see note 25).

The exit bonds used in this illustration were designed to achieve the same negative resource transfer in the short run as the Baker Plan. Even to accomplish this, the nonexiting banks will have to be prepared to increase their new lending by 50 percent, from 2.5 percent to 3.75 percent of exposure each year, to compensate for the banks that exit. If that is judged impractical within the process of assembling new money packages, or if it is concluded that the negative resource transfer implied by the Baker Plan is unacceptably large and that the banks should play a role in reducing it, then it might be necessary to supplement voluntary debt relief with a reconstruction of the debt of the nonexiting banks. It was suggested in section 5 that such a reconstruction might provide for automatic rollover of principal and capitalization of interest when debt-service charges exceed a cap based on export earnings.

These figures make it clear that voluntary debt relief is no panacea. If the debt crisis evaporates quickly and painlessly in the next five years, it will be because the value of debtor-country exports surges as the higher recent primary product prices stabilize, or because interest rates halve again without a deterioration in the debtors' terms of trade. If a new upsurge in interest rates causes a new recession, then voluntary debt relief is not likely to counter the damage. But it could nonetheless play a useful role in intermediate scenarios in which world growth is maintained in the range of 2 percent or 3 percent per year with no decisive changes in interest rates and some relapse in the terms of trade. It could also have some psychological importance in reassuring debtors that the costs of past overborrowing (equals overlending) are being shared. And it would offer assurance that their longer-run position will improve even if export performance continues to be disappointing.

7 *Conclusion*

An end to the debt crisis implies two things. The first is an easing of the foreign exchange constraint that has throttled growth in the debtor countries since 1982. The second is an end to the repeated need to negotiate external financial support in a crisis atmosphere.

Voluntary debt relief alone could probably achieve both eventually, but the import of table 2 is that the process could be lengthy. A more rapid solution requires the provision of routine liquidity relief according to need. This would seem to demand either substantially larger lending by the multilateral development banks, one of the comprehensive schemes for debt relief whose practicality was questioned in section 2, or else a combination of voluntary debt relief with the cap plus capitalization proposal developed at the end of section 5. My own preference is for the latter solution.

The virtue of the Baker Plan is its elasticity, which has already proved sufficient to embrace the menu approach. The proposals developed in this study seek to carry this process of evolutionary change a stage further. They seek not so much to lengthen the menu as to provide a greater contrast in the entrées that will induce each bank to make a clear decision as to whether its contribution will take the form of debt relief or liquidity relief. They envisage a bold but temporary use of the World Bank's guarantee powers as the public sector's contribution to presenting the banks with a sharp choice concerning the form in which each will contribute. To the debtor countries they offer both assurance of light at the end of the tunnel and the hope of a shorter tunnel.

Appendix

Evaluating the Mexican Defeasance Scheme

The Mexican defeasance scheme involves Mexico using dollars from its reserves in order to buy US Treasury zero-coupon bonds that will be worth about five times their current cost in the year 2008, when they mature. Using these as collateral for the principal, Mexico then issues bonds with a face value equal to the maturity value of the zero-coupon bonds. Each $1 million of these bonds is exchanged for $(1/*b*) million of old loans, where *b* is a price that the banks bid for the swap. The bid price *b* is equal to one minus the discount at which the banks offer to trade in their old debt for new bonds—for example, a 40 percent discount is equivalent to a bid price *b* of 0.6. The lower the bid price (and the greater the discount), the larger are the savings to Mexico.

The annual cash-flow saving (C_b, measured in millions of dollars) to Mexico from issuing $1 million of such bonds is given by the formula

$$C_b = i/b - (i + r) - 0.2u$$

where *i* is the interest rate Mexico pays on the existing debt (LIBOR plus a margin of 0.8125 percent), *r* is a premium of 0.8125 percent on the margin that will be paid on the bonds, and *u* is the US interest rate that would have been earned on the reserves used to buy zero-coupon bonds had they not been used for that purpose.[1] Mexico gets the additional benefit at the end of 20 years of extinguishing $1 million of its debt. (It would be double-counting to include both the cash-flow benefit and *immediate* extinction of the debt.)

1. It might be argued that the relevant alternative use of reserves is to spend them on increased imports of capital goods rather than to hold them, in which case both defeasance and buybacks appear less attractive to the debtor (though their *relative* merits are unaffected, since the comparison involves a given outlay of foreign exchange).

Using the values of these variables on 22 March 1988 (LIBOR = 0.06875, i = 0.076875, r = 0.008125, and u = 0.0589), one can calculate the cash-flow saving from issuing $1 billion of bonds as follows:

b	0.5	0.6	0.7	0.78
C_b ($ million)	57.0	31.3	13.0	1.8

Thus for bids above 78 cents on the dollar, Mexico would have received no cash-flow benefit from a swap for the next 20 years (although it would still have gained the benefit of extinguishing debt 20 years in the future). In fact, the bids that were accepted averaged 70 cents on the dollar, so that actual cash-flow savings will be $13 million per billion dollars of new bonds issued, or about $33 million in total. It may also be noted that the benefit of the swaps increases with higher interest charges (i) and decreases with a higher premium (r) and US interest rate (u).

The Mexican scheme can be contrasted with the use of a part of Mexico's reserves equal to the expenditure on zero-coupon bonds to buy back debt on the secondary market. Let the price on the secondary market be s, expressed as a fraction (cents per dollar of debt), equal to one minus the discount. Then the use of $0.2 billion of reserves to buy back debt will lead to a cash-flow saving C_s:

$$C_s = \$(0.2i/s - 0.2u) \text{ billion}$$

and will also have extinguished $(0.2/$s$) billion of debt in 20 years' time. The current value of Mexican debt on the secondary market is about 0.5, which indicates that $0.2 billion could have bought $19 million per annum of interest relief had it been applied to a buyback program instead of a swap program (or somewhat less if Mexican purchases had pushed the price up). This is somewhat larger than the $13 million of interest relief achieved by the defeasance alternative, but the buyback alternative would have brought only $0.4 billion of principal reduction, rather than the $1 billion of the swap program.

Whether Mexico should prefer a swap program to the buyback alternative depends on a comparison between the greater interest savings under buybacks and the greater principal reduction under swaps. Such a comparison requires the introduction of the rate (d) at which Mexico discounts future foreign-exchange savings. Specifically, swaps will be preferred if the present value of \$600 million of savings in 2008 is greater than that of a stream of interest savings of \$6 million per year spread over the next 20 years. The discount rate that equates these two present values is just under 14 percent per year. For lower discount rates, defeasance is preferable; for higher discount rates, buybacks are preferable.

What would be a reasonable value for d, the rate at which a country like Mexico should discount future foreign-exchange availability? A figure of 10 percent, or 0.10, is often used as a social discount rate. A country undertaking a program to improve its balance of payments expects foreign exchange to become less of a constraint over time, which implies that the social discount rate applicable to foreign exchange should be higher than that which applies to resources in general. A figure of at least 0.12 and probably as much as 0.15 might be reasonable. In the light of this it is questionable whether the use of foreign exchange to buy zero-coupon bonds in order to defease debt was more cost-efficient than a buyback program would have been.

We now turn to an analysis of the interests of the creditors, the banks, in choosing between the options of:

- holding on to their existing loans
- selling loans on the secondary market
- swapping loans into principal-collateralized bonds.

If bankers were confident that they would receive all their scheduled debt-service payments, they would choose to hold on to their existing loans. Hence in order to compare their incentive to sell or swap them rather than to hold on one needs to model their expectations of receiving future debt-service payments. It seems reasonable to assume that they expect the principal on their outstanding loans to be rolled over indefinitely. Perhaps the most natural assumption, which also has the virtue of being analytically tractable, is that their expectation of receiving interest is constant over time. In order to check that the results are not unduly sensitive to this assumption, two alternatives are also investigated. The three assumptions considered are:

A. that they expect to receive interest in any period with some constant probability, p

B. that their expectation of receiving interest in year t is v^t, where v is a number between zero and one, so that their hopes of receiving interest decrease asymptotically toward zero as time progresses

C. that some fraction n of the interest due will have to be capitalized (or re-lent each year as new money).

The present value of holding on to a loan, discounting at the interest rate i, in the first case is:

$$PVL_A = pi/(1+i) + pi/(1+i)^2 + \ldots = p$$

which is, as expected, equal to 1 when $p = 1$.[2]

In the second case,

$$PVL_B = iv/(1+i) + iv^2/(1+i)^2 + \ldots = iv/(1+i-v)$$

which is equal to 1 when $v = 1$.

In the third case,

$$PVL_C = (1-n)i/(1+i) + (1-n)i/(1+i)^2 + \ldots = 1 - n$$

which is equal to 1 when $n = 0$. Note that the first and third cases are analytically identical: to be sure of receiving $(1-n)i$ in perpetuity is equivalent to expecting to receive $p = (1-n)$ of the interest i on average.

The present value of a sale on the secondary market is simply:

$$PVS = s.$$

The present value of swapping into bonds is:

$$PVB = b\left[\sum_{t=1}^{20} \frac{(i + r)q_t}{(1 + i)^t} + \frac{1}{(1 + i)^{20}}\right]$$

2. It could be argued that the banks' appropriate discount rate is their cost of funds, LIBOR, without addition of the spread. The present value of making a riskless loan would then be strictly positive.

where q_t is the probability the banker attaches to the interest due in year t being paid. Interest, unlike principal (which is collateralized), is still subject to country risk, and hence interest payments have to be multiplied by the probability that they will actually be received.

One can again make two assumptions about the probability of receiving interest: that it is constant over time, and that it decreases asymptotically. If the bonds are treated as senior to existing debt, then $q > p$ in case A or $q > v$ in case B; if not, $q = p$ or $q = v$, respectively.

A rational banker will presumably choose the option that maximizes the present value of his expected future receipts.[3] (Any personal inclination he might have to be charitable to his Third World clients is liable to be constrained by the threat of legal action by shareholders.) Hence in case A he would hold on to his loans rather than sell them on the secondary market if

$$PVL_A > PVS,$$

i.e., if $p > s$. Bankers who are willing to sell on the secondary market at the current price of $s = 0.5$ thus appear to believe that there is no more than a 50 percent probability that they will actually receive their due interest payments in any future year. Alternatively, recalling the equivalence of cases A and C, they may believe that they will be required to capitalize one-half of the interest due in perpetuity (or provide the equivalent in the form of new money).

In case B, the banker will hold on to his loans rather than sell on the secondary market if

$$PVL_B > PVS,$$

i.e., if $iv/(1 + i - v) > s$. For the values $i = 0.076875$, $s = 0.5$, taken previously, this implies that he will sell on the secondary market if and only if $v < 0.933$.

The choice between holding on to loans or selling on the secondary market is shown by the vertical lines at $p = 0.5$ and $v = 0.93$ for cases A and B respectively in figures A.1 and A.2. To the right of those lines, the banker will hold on to his loans; to the left, he will sell on the secondary market.

3. Portfolio theory might suggest that a banker would prefer to hold a mix of the different assets, but this is relevant only when the bank holds a significant fraction of its assets in claims against a single country.

FIGURE A.1
The bankers' choice with constant default probability and no seniority

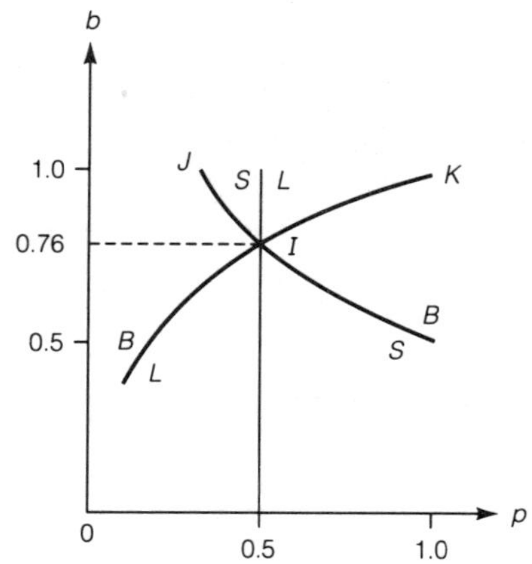

FIGURE A.2
The bankers' choice with increasing default probability and no seniority

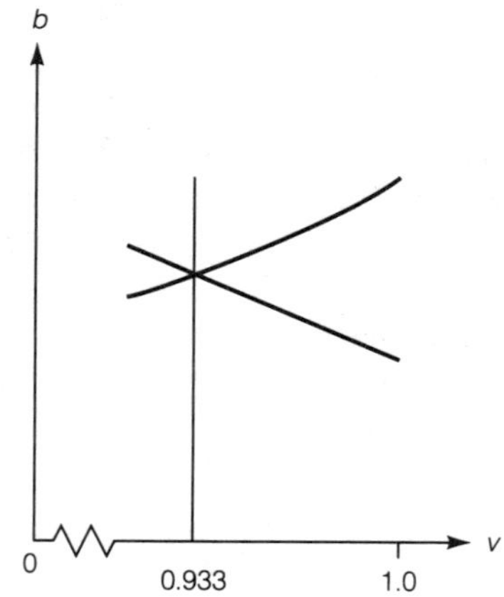

FIGURE A.3
The bankers' choice with constant default probability on loans and no default probability on bonds

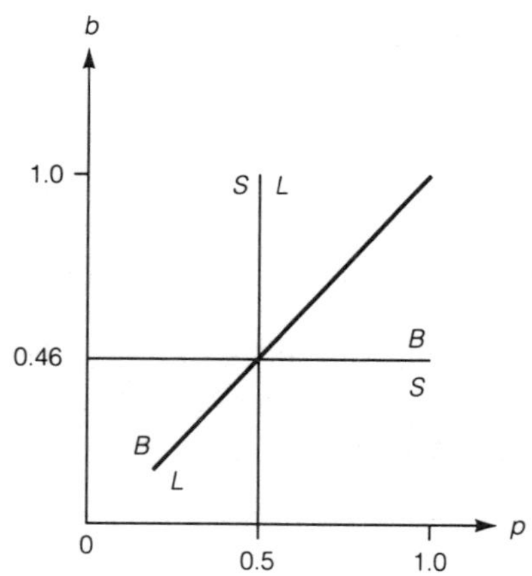

FIGURE A.4
The bankers' choice with constant default probability on loans and seniority for bond interest

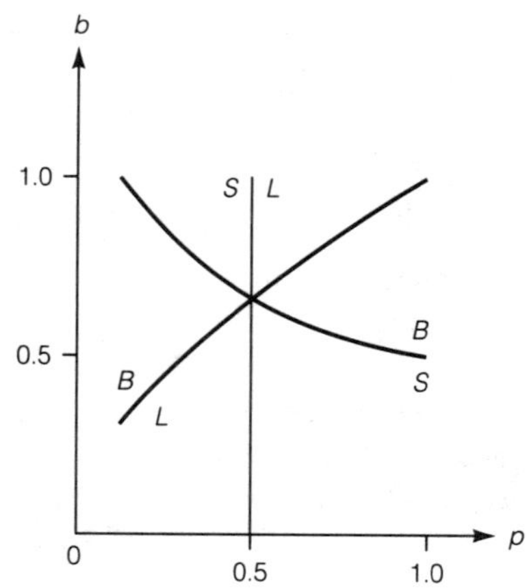

Comparing defeasance with sales on the secondary market is more difficult, since the value of *PVB* depends on *b* and *q* as well as *i* and *r*. Using the same values of *i* and *r* as before, table A.1 shows *PVB* (the expected present value to the bank of swapping $1 million of its loans into collateralized bonds) as a function of *b* (the bid price for the swap) and *q*, where $q_t = p$ (i.e., constant default probability, no seniority). Since *PVS* = 0.5, *PVB* is greater than *PVS* for relatively high combinations of *q* (=*p*) and *b*. The boundary where *PVB* = *PVS* is shown as the downward sloping line from *J* in figure A.1, where the banker will choose to buy bonds above the line and to sell on the secondary market below it, as indicated by the letters '*B*' and '*S*' on each side of the line.

TABLE A.1 **PVB with constant default probability** (thousand dollars)

b	*q*			
	0.25	*0.5*	*0.75*	*1.0*
0.4	176	262	347	433
0.5	220	327	434	541
0.6	265	393	521	649
0.7	309	458	608	757
0.8	353	524	694	865
0.9	397	589	781	973
1.0	441	655	868	1082

Note: Calculated using i = 0.076875 and r = 0.008125. PVB is the present value to a bank of swapping $1 million of loans into collateralized bonds.

TABLE A.2 **PVB with increasing default probability** (thousand dollars)

b	*q*			
	0.9	*0.933*	*0.95*	*1.0*
0.4	259	299	325	433
0.5	324	374	406	541
0.6	389	448	487	649
0.7	454	523	568	757
0.8	518	598	650	865

Note: Calculated using i = 0.076875 and r = 0.008125. PVB is the present value to a bank of swapping $1 million of loans into collateralized bonds.

Similarly, the present value of swapping into bonds is shown in table A.2 as a function of b and q for the case where $q_t = v^t$ (i.e., perception of increasing default probability and no seniority). Since *PVS* is still 0.5, *PVB* is again greater than *PVS* for relatively high combinations of q $(=v)$ and b. The boundary where $PVB = PVS$ is shown as the downward-sloping line in figure A.2. The banker will choose to sell on the secondary market below that line and to swap into bonds above it.

Consider next the choice between swapping and selling in the case where interest on the defeased bonds is believed by the banker to have seniority over interest on loans. Consider in particular the extreme case where default probability on bond interest is considered to be zero, i.e., $q = 1$. Then *PVB* is a function of b alone. Hence the boundary where $PVB = PVS$ is a horizontal line (figure A.3). It is interesting to note that the critical value of b is actually less than 0.5; a price even lower than that on the secondary market is justified by the premium on the bond's interest rate.

In the case where interest on the collateralized bonds is regarded as senior to that on loans, but still risky, the line $PVB = PVS$ is rotated upwards around the point ($p = 1.0$, $b = 0.46$) to some level intermediate between the case shown in figure A.1 and that shown in figure A.3, as shown in figure A.4.

One could repeat the analysis of seniority for bond interest for the case where default risk is perceived to increase over time, but the results are similar and so the analysis is omitted.

Finally, it is necessary to compare *PVL* and *PVB*—the expected profitability of holding on to loans versus swapping into collateralized bonds. In case A, where default probability is constant, and with no seniority for bond interest, $PVL = p$. *PVB* also increases as q $(=p)$ does, so that the locus in figure A.1, where $PVL = PVB$, is upward sloping. In fact it cuts the intersection of the other two lines. Swapping into bonds is more profitable above that line, and holding on to loans is preferred below it.

The same is easily seen to be true in the other three cases represented in figures A.2, A.3, and A.4.

Comparing all three alternatives, it can be seen that the option of holding on to loans dominates the other two options in the southeast quadrant of figure A.1 (the quadrant *KIH*). Similarly, the option of selling on the secondary market dominates in the southwest quadrant *JIH*. Swapping into collateralized bonds dominates in the northern quadrant *JIK*. The same is true in the other three figures. The preferred options are summarized in figure 1 in the text.

In figures A.1 and A.2, where bond interest does not enjoy seniority, the least that the banks could have been expected to bid to swap into collateralized bonds was 0.76. In contrast, they might have bid as low as 0.46 in the case of no default probability, shown in figure A.3, or at some intermediate level in the case of seniority, shown in figure A.4. According to press reports, some differences of view were expressed prior to the bidding for the Mexican bonds as to whether they would carry seniority or not, with Mexican officials implying that they would and both Morgan Guaranty and the US Treasury denying this. The fact that the accepted bids averaged 0.7 strongly suggests that the banks placed rather limited value on the Mexican assertions.

The analysis thus reveals two cases in which Mexico would seem able to gain more through the defeasance scheme than it could have done through a buyback program. One is if the rate at which Mexico discounts foreign exchange is set relatively low. The other is if defeasance is made more attractive to the banks by making the interest payments on the bonds senior to those on the old loans.

References

Bergsten, C. Fred, William R. Cline and John Williamson. 1985. *Bank Lending to Developing Countries: The Policy Alternatives,* POLICY ANALYSES IN INTERNATIONAL ECONOMICS 10. Washington: Institute for International Economics.

Bulow, Jeremy, and Kenneth Rogoff. 1988. "Sovereign Debt Restructuring: Panacea or Pangloss?" Unpublished paper. Photocopy.

Cline, William R. 1984. *International Debt: Systemic Risk and Policy Response.* Washington: Institute for International Economics.

———. 1987. *Mobilizing Bank Lending to Developing Countries,* POLICY ANALYSES IN INTERNATIONAL ECONOMICS 18. Washington: Institute for International Economics.

Cohen, Benjamin J. 1988. *The Political Economy of LDC Debt.* Unpublished paper, Fletcher School of Law and Diplomacy, Tufts University. Photocopy.

Cohen, Daniel. 1985. "How to Evaluate the Solvency of an Indebted Nation." *Economic Policy* (November).

Corden, W. Max. 1988. "Debt Relief and Adjustment Incentives: A Theoretical Explanation." Unpublished paper, IMF. Photocopy.

Dooley, Michael P. 1988a. "Buy-backs and the Market Valuation of External Debt." IMF *Staff Papers.* June.

———. 1988b. "Analysis of Self-financed Buy-backs and Asset Exchanges." IMF *Working Paper.*

Eaton, Jonathan, Mark Gersovitz, and Joseph E. Stiglitz. 1986. "The Pure Theory of Country Risk." *European Economic Review.*

Eichengreen, Barry and Richard Portes. 1988. "Settling Defaults in the Era of Bond Finance." Paper presented to the conference on "A Long-run Perspective on the Debt Crisis." San Francisco, May.

Froot, Kenneth A. 1988. "Buy-backs, Exit Bonds, and the Optimality of Debt and Liquidity Relief." Unpublished paper, Sloan School of Management, Massachusetts Institute of Technology. Photocopy.

Islam, Shafiqul. 1988. *Breaking the International Debt Deadlock.* Council on Foreign Relations.

Ize, Alain and Guillermo Ortiz. 1987. "Fiscal Rigidities, Public Debt, and Capital Flight." IMF *Staff Papers* (June).

Jorgensen, Erika and Jeffrey Sachs. 1988. "The Costs of Default: The Settlement of Interwar Loans to Latin America." Paper presented to the conference on "A Long-Run Perspective on the Debt Crisis." San Francisco, May.

Kaletsky, Anatole. 1985. *The Costs of Default.* New York: Twentieth Century Fund.

Kenen, Peter B. 1983. "Third World Debt: Sharing the Burden, a Bailout Plan for the Banks." *New York Times,* 6 March.

Krugman, Paul R. 1988a. "Financing versus Forgiving a Debt Overhang." *NBER Working Paper* 2486.

———. 1988b. "Market-based Debt-reduction Schemes." *NBER Working Paper* 2587. (To appear in Frenkel, Jacob A., ed. *Analytic Issues in Debt.* Washington: International Monetary Fund. Forthcoming.)

LaFalce, John. 1987. "Third World Debt Crisis: The Urgent Need to Confront Reality." Statement in Washington, 5 March.

Lessard, Donald R. and John Williamson. 1985. *Financial Intermediation Beyond the Debt Crisis,* POLICY ANALYSES IN INTERNATIONAL ECONOMICS 12. Washington: Institute for International Economics.

Pease, Don. 1988. "A Congressional Plan to Solve the Debt Crisis." *The International Economy* (March/April).

Portes, Richard. 1987. "Debt and the Market." Paper presented to the Group of Thirty. Photocopy.

Roberts, David L., and Eli M. Remolona. 1987. "Debt Swaps: A Technique in Developing Country Finance." In *Finance for Developing Countries,* edited by R. A. Debs, D. L. Roberts, and E.M. Remolona. New York: Group of Thirty.

Robinson, James D. III. 1988. "A Comprehensive Agenda for LDC Debt and World Trade Growth." Speech before the Overseas Development Council, 29 February.

Rohatyn, Felix G. 1983. "A Plan for Stretching Out Global Debt." *Business Week,* 28 February.

Rotberg, Eugene H. 1988. *Toward A Solution to the Debt Crisis,* Merill Lynch and Co.

Sachs, Jeffrey. 1986. "The Debt Overhang Problem of Developing Countries." Paper presented at the conference in memory of Carlos Diaz-Alejandro, Helsinki.

———. 1988. "Conditionality, Debt Relief, and the Developing Country Debt Crisis." Unpublished paper. Photocopy.

Sachs, Jeffrey, and Harry Huizinga. 1987. "US Commercial Banks and the Developing-Country Debt Crisis." *Brookings Papers on Economic Activity* 2.

Sengupta, Arjun K. 1988. "A Proposal for a Debt Adjustment Facility." Unpublished paper. Photocopy.

Summit Communiqué. 1988. IMF Survey. Vol. 17, No. 13, *Leaders of Group of 7 Countries Adopt Debt Plan to Help Poorest.* Washington, D.C.: International Monetary Fund, 1988.

Wallich, Henry C. 1943. "The Future of Latin American Dollar Bonds." *American Economic Review* (June)

Williamson, John. 1984. "On the Question of Debt Relief." Appendix to the Statement of the Roundtable on Money and Finance, New York, 13–14 December. Islamabad: North–South Roundtable.

World Debt Tables. 1988. Volume 1. Washington: World Bank.

Key to Notation

a	amortization rate
b	bid price on loan/bond swap (defeasance)
B_t	debt-service obligation in year t
C_b	annual cash-flow saving to debtor from defeasing bonds
C_s	annual cash-flow saving to debtor from repurchasing in secondary market
C_t	debt service change in year t
d	debtor country's social discount rate for foreign exchange
D_t	value of outstanding debt in year t
i	interest rate paid by debtor to banks on existing loans, equal to LIBOR plus spread
n	constant fraction of interest due that banks expect to capitalize in case C
p_t	bankers' perception of (constant) probability of receiving interest in case A (constant default probability)
P_t	debt-service payments due in year t
q_t	bankers' perception of probability that interest will be paid on collateralized bonds in year t
r	interest premium paid on defeased bonds
s	price of loans on secondary market
S_t	surplus available for debt service in year t
t	time
u	US interest rate earned by debtor country on its reserves
v^t	bankers' perception of probability that interest will be paid in case B (increasing default probability)
X	exports
PVB	expected present discounted value of collateralized bonds
PVL	expected present discounted value of holding on to loans
PVS	expected present discounted value of sales on secondary market

Other Publications from the Institute

POLICY ANALYSES IN INTERNATIONAL ECONOMICS SERIES

1 **The Lending Policies of the International Monetary Fund**
John Williamson/August 1982

2 **"Reciprocity": A New Approach to World Trade Policy?**
William R. Cline/September 1982

3 **Trade Policy in the 1980s**
C. Fred Bergsten and William R. Cline/November 1982

4 **International Debt and the Stability of the World Economy**
William R. Cline/September 1983

5 **The Exchange Rate System, Second Edition**
John Williamson/September 1983, rev. June 1985

6 **Economic Sanctions in Support of Foreign Policy Goals**
Gary Clyde Hufbauer and Jeffrey J. Schott/October 1983

7 **A New SDR Allocation?**
John Williamson/March 1984

8 **An International Standard for Monetary Stabilization**
Ronald I. McKinnon/March 1984

9 **The Yen/Dollar Agreement: Liberalizing Japanese Capital Markets**
Jeffrey A. Frankel/December 1984

10 **Bank Lending to Developing Countries: The Policy Alternatives**
C. Fred Bergsten, William R. Cline, and John Williamson/April 1985

11 **Trading for Growth: The Next Round of Trade Negotiations**
Gary Clyde Hufbauer and Jeffrey J. Schott/September 1985

12 **Financial Intermediation Beyond the Debt Crisis**
Donald R. Lessard and John Williamson/September 1985

13 **The United States–Japan Economic Problem**
C. Fred Bergsten and William R. Cline/October 1985, rev. January 1987

14 **Deficits and the Dollar: The World Economy at Risk**
Stephen Marris/December 1985, rev. November 1987

15 **Trade Policy for Troubled Industries**
Gary Clyde Hufbauer and Howard F. Rosen/March 1986

16 **The United States and Canada: The Quest for Free Trade**
Paul Wonnacott, with an Appendix by *John Williamson*/March 1987

17 **Adjusting to Success: Balance of Payments Policy in the East Asian NICs**
Bela Balassa and John Williamson/June 1987

18 **Mobilizing Bank Lending to Debtor Countries**
William R. Cline/June 1987

19 **Auction Quotas and United States Trade Policy**
C. Fred Bergsten, Kimberly Ann Elliott, Jeffrey J. Schott, and Wendy E. Takacs/September 1987

20 **Agriculture and the GATT: Rewriting the Rules**
Dale E. Hathaway/September 1987

21 **Anti-Protection: Changing Forces in United States Trade Politics**
I. M. Destler and John S. Odell/September 1987

22 **Targets and Indicators: A Blueprint for the International Coordination of Economic Policy**
John Williamson and Marcus H. Miller/September 1987

23 **Capital Flight: The Problem and Policy Responses**
Donald R. Lessard and John Williamson/December 1987

24 **United States–Canada Free Trade: An Evaluation of the Agreement**
Jeffrey J. Schott/April 1988

25 **Voluntary Approaches to Debt Relief**
John Williamson/September 1988

BOOKS

IMF Conditionality
John Williamson, editor/1983

Trade Policy in the 1980s
William R. Cline, editor/1983

Subsidies in International Trade
Gary Clyde Hufbauer and Joanna Shelton Erb/1984

International Debt: Systemic Risk and Policy Response
William R. Cline/1984

Economic Sanctions Reconsidered: History and Current Policy
Gary Clyde Hufbauer and Jeffrey J. Schott, assisted by Kimberly Ann Elliott/1985

Trade Protection in the United States: 31 Case Studies
Gary Clyde Hufbauer, Diane T. Berliner, and Kimberly Ann Elliott/1986

Toward Renewed Economic Growth in Latin America
Bela Balassa, Gerardo M. Bueno, Pedro-Pablo Kuczynski, and Mario Henrique Simonsen/1986

American Trade Politics: System Under Stress
I. M. Destler/1986

The Future of World Trade in Textiles and Apparel
William R. Cline/1987

Capital Flight and Third World Debt
Donald R. Lessard and John Williamson, editors/1987

The Canada–United States Free Trade Agreement: The Global Impact
Jeffrey J. Schott and Murray G. Smith, editors/1988

Managing the Dollar: From the Plaza to the Louvre
Yoichi Funabashi/1988

Reforming World Agricultural Trade
Twenty-nine Professionals from Seventeen Countries/1988

World Agricultural Trade: Building a Consensus
William M. Miner and Dale E. Hathaway, editors/1988

Japan in the World Economy
Bela Balassa and Marcus Noland/1988

SPECIAL REPORTS

1 **Promoting World Recovery: A Statement on Global Economic Strategy**
by Twenty-six Economists from Fourteen Countries/December 1982

2 **Prospects for Adjustment in Argentina, Brazil, and Mexico: Responding to the Debt Crisis**
John Williamson, editor/June 1983

3 **Inflation and Indexation: Argentina, Brazil, and Israel**
John Williamson, editor/March 1985

4 **Global Economic Imbalances**
C. Fred Bergsten, editor/March 1986

5 **African Debt and Financing**
Carol Lancaster and John Williamson, editors/May 1986

6 **Resolving the Global Economic Crisis: After Wall Street**
Thirty-three Economists from Thirteen Countries/December 1987

7 **World Economic Problems**
Kimberly Ann Elliott and John Williamson, editors/April 1988

FORTHCOMING

The United States as a Debtor Country
C. Fred Bergsten and Shafiqul Islam

Domestic Adjustment and International Trade
Gary Clyde Hufbauer and Howard F. Rosen, editors

United States External Adjustment and the World Economy
William R. Cline and Stephen Marris

Energy Policy for the 1990s: A Global Perspective
Philip K. Verleger, Jr.

The Outlook for World Commodity Prices
Philip K. Verleger, Jr.

Economic Relations Between the United States and Korea: Conflict or Cooperation?
Thomas O. Bayard and Soo-Gil Young, editors

International Economic Policy for the New Administration
C. Fred Bergsten

Exchange Rate Policy Making in the United States
I. M. Destler and C. Randall Henning

Equilibrium Exchange Rates: An Update
John Williamson

Foreign Direct Investment in the United States
Edward M. Graham and Paul R. Krugman

The Politics of International Monetary Cooperation
C. Fred Bergsten, I. M. Destler, C. Randall Henning, and John Williamson

The International Monetary Fund: The Record and the Prospects
C. David Finch

Reciprocity and Retaliation: An Evaluation of Aggressive Trade Policies
Thomas O. Bayard

More Free Trade Areas?
Jeffrey J. Schott

Oil Crisis Intervention: A Blueprint for International Cooperation
Philip K. Verleger, Jr.

Pacific Area Trade: Threat or Opportunity for the United States?
Bela Balassa and Marcus Noland

Third World Debt: A Reappraisal
William R. Cline